Many Lovers

Book 4267

Volume 1

Many Lovers

Book 4267

Volume 1

Harriet Gore

A publication of Touch LOVE Worldwide

Published by Touch Love Worldwide Ltd.

MANY LOVERS
BOOK 4267
VOLUME 1

A publication of Touch LOVE Worldwide

ISBN 978-0-993-14840-8

Contents

Something in the dark was calling out for me
I called on my camera to answer the call
What it saw is what you see – *Harriet Gore*

Title "**MANY LOVERS**" suggested by William Gore

UNEDITED

This is me. Unedited. I give you me. Make of me what you may.

Harriet Gore

BOOK 0
THE LONGEST BOOK

LOVE

BOOK 1

THE LIFE OF AN IDEA

This question has been occupying me and I would like us to discuss it. Do you think that you and I started life as ideas, striking and bouncing around in space?

Look at that backpack over there, enjoying the ride on that back. Feeling content that it has come to be. Pampered and cherished journeying on the back. Look at that shoe and that coat and that shirt. All on their moving mannequins. Going up the escalator on a free ride. Just as they are. Just as conceived? Human beings. Idea bearers? Human beings. Models of ideas? Modelling ideas? Look at that house and that hat and that hut. They are beings, just as they are.

Do you think ideas choose targets to strike? Or could it be that it is the targets which choose and target the ideas? Or are ideas striking indiscriminately and randomly and hitting targets by chance?

Does an idea choose to strike the greatest ambitious builder within its striking distance, the builder best positioned to bring the idea to a life of greatness, to exhibit it so that others can see, to make it as successful as it can be?

Do you think that every being is an idea propelled by ideas, some more powerful than others, some more dominating than others seeking to dominate all, some ideas recruiting other ideas to suppress some ideas and promote other ideas?

Do you think it is an idea that transforms its builder from being unknown to being known, from being ordinary to being extraordinary, from being a nonentity to being a towering greatness? Are there queues of ideas waiting to strike the greatest skilled and talented builders, stirring the passion in the strongest builders so that they will bring them to life in a grand style? Is there a limit to the growth and expansion of a particular idea?

What is success in the life of an idea? When is an idea as successful as it can be?

Do you think the world itself is an idea or that the idea is the world, the world of ideas or the idea of worlds, a world pregnant with ideas or a world delivered by ideas?

When an idea strikes you or comes visiting you, are you obliged to keep the idea and build it or build on it? How do you know if it is an idea you should build on or one which will build you or one which will destroy you? Where an idea strikes but does not take root, how do you know if it is the idea which left you or if you are the one who did not keep the idea?

Well this is my own idea. You are an idea. I am an idea. A thing is an idea. Everything is an idea. One thing is an idea. Everyone is an idea. Anything is an idea. Many things are ideas. All things are ideas. Nothing itself is an idea. Nothingness an idea. Some ideas are limiting. Some ideas are limited. Some ideas are limitless. Some ideas are enslaving. Some ideas are liberating. Some expand endlessly. Some ideas change some. Some ideas build some. Some build on some ideas. Some ideas destroy some. Some destroy some ideas. Some ideas visit and stay. Some strike and move on. Some ideas are actually on strike. You wrestle to keep some. Some wrestle to keep you.

Some ideas strike and control the struck and the struck is left with no choice but to be the channel of the idea and manifest the idea. Some ideas are not so controlling but leaves the struck with a choice.

You see my dear friend, I think of myself as an idea which struck my creator. No one ever asked whether I chose my creator. So I am asking myself that question. I know who I am told my creator is. I accept what I'm told. But how can I be sure of what happened before I became?

My creator is sure and those who witnessed the process of creation are sure too. So I have been riding on their surety to be sure that my creator is my parent. But is my parent sure of who I am and all I am? My creator may be sure of how I was made visible and tangible but is that all I am?

I have been observing dad and mum at work. They create all the time in that work space. The process I witness reveals how I may have come to be. First, as a thought which powered an action. But did I plant the thought by striking my creator with the idea of me? Did I inspire my creator to bring to life the idea of me or did the thought of me just appear from nowhere to start occupying my creator? Did I choose my parent to be my creator, then stirred my creator's spirit to move and to create what I have become? Or did my parent do it all by own self with no input at all from me? Is my parent and I a team working together at all times? These questions have been occupying me.

One thing is for sure. At the time I occupied my parent's thoughts, I lived within the confines of my parent's thoughts except when my parent shared own thoughts with others. At the time my creator was creating the image of me, I was visible to my creator but invisible to others except in so far as my creator made me visible to others. From nothingness to something else. From intangible formless, my parent's action created tangible form. My creator and I experienced the journey. From roll of canvas to a cut of canvas, from blank stretched to the first touch of paint. My creator and I were together from beginning to the end, expanding and changing until we have purged ourselves as best as we could at the time we did.

But it was not just my creator and I, there were others too, though they remained unseen; the canvas maker, the paint maker, the brush maker, the transporters and all the others. From beginning until now, the experience has been a constant change. First, from nothingness which cannot be seen. Then to something which can be seen and touched. This something itself has been changing from moment to moment from day to day. This is why I ask: How do I look? I do not know how I look. If I meet myself, I will not recognise me. Please tell me what you see.

BOOK 2

HOW DO I LOOK?

When my parent was creating me, there were many spirits at play. I experienced the air, its spirit caressed me, the wind blew by, its effect changed a number of things and its spirit moved me. The sunray touched and stayed, its spirit dwelt in me. In my creator and around my creator, the spirits played their parts. The incredible forces of the earth did not want to be left out, so all the elements came out and fully joined in. With a mind of their own, they generously added themselves to what's on their path. My creator was on their path and so was I, and I remain on their path.

The air gave generously and got mixed in. The sun rayed generously to become part of me. At night the moon visited whilst my creator slept, its beautiful changing face beamed all night as it kept watch. It was a keen observer and did not miss a thing. So we would converse until the morning comes on its shift. What no one knew is that the moon knew what my creator did not know and continued to smile at the thought of all it witnessed happening around me. My creator was in the dark, what some call sleep, but the dark was in me, surrounded me, highlighting the light.

You see my dear friend, the elements in me are more than the visible materials my creator used to make me. I was present in the spirits of both what my creator saw and what my creator did not see and those spirits are in me. Some spirits were in my creator's thoughts and some came from my creator's experience. So spirits are part of my big family. The spirits influential at the time dad was creating me, became part of me. What you now see is bigger than what was in my creator's thoughts. So this is why I ask: How do I look?

My creator and I experienced a constant change, so I do not know how I look. Can you see all the spirits and all the elements in me? Please tell me what you see. How do I look?

Some think that I started life as cut bunch of sunflowers but how did the cut bunch of sunflowers start life. For those who think I started life as cut sunflower, they are right to think that from the seen, I became unseen and from the unseen, I became the seen but is that the whole story? Is that the only story? Did I really start life as cut sunflower? Is that who I am? Your own premise may be that I was first unseen then became a vision from which I was made into the seen which you now see though part of me may still remain unseen. But how does that unseen which became a vision look? Does it look like I look?

You see my dear friend, at conception, I lived inside my creator, but now, it is I, who bear my creator. I bear my creator's name. In me my creator and I meet, but I don't know if my creator and I look alike. I still do not know how I look for I have never seen myself and not sure how my creator looks though I have been told a name and bear the name. A lot of things joined forces to become me and the me I became is encountering more forces and the forces I am absorbing are keeping me in constant change. Please tell me what you see. How do I look?

BOOK 3

THE ORIGINAL IDEA

What's your name? You ask
 What's in a name? My thought
 'Am I in a name?
 Is a name in me?
 A name could be anything, everything or nothing at all.
 You did not hear my thoughts so you asked me once again, and made me think aloud…
 I have not made a name, so I cannot tell a name
 I get to share a name only when I've made a name.
 You heard that thought and said
 "How can that be?
 You must have a name
 Every being has a name
 Please tell me your name"
 Where I come from, I thought out loud, *we make a name ourselves. So I'm here to make a name but have not quite made it. The name I want to make is the name I want to be. A special kind of name. A unique name for me. A name which tells all, everything about me. To make such a name, I must first know myself. For me to know myself, I must first find myself. For me to find myself, I must first recognise myself, go on adventures, fall to rise, learn to unlearn, know the strength in weak, to know the weak in strength.*

9

An adventure produces a name, delivers a name, wakes up names. An adventure draws out names, invokes a name and brings out names. I'm here to wake my name, know my name to call my name.

There are many names in me but I do not know them yet. There are so many things about me which remain unknown to me. I don't even know how I look. No mirrors tell me enough. When the mirrors called humans look into me, they call me 'colourful', 'beautiful', one 'ful', another 'ful', which, of course, does not tell me very much. But you are different. You have not called me any 'ful'. You have not called me any name. Rather you ask me my name, making me think and speak. You engage in conversation which reminds me that I am on adventure. An adventurous journey to know who I am, what I am and why I am.

'What's your name' you asked. 'Come with me' I say. I like your company and would like you to come with me, so together we would discover that which I do not know. Together, both of us can find my name. I like your companionship because at the outset, you caught my eye.

You saw me from a distance and stirred and steered towards me. Your thoughts attracted me. I was strongly drawn to you and then became struck. Struck by the way you looked at me. Not just on the surface but deep into me. Struck by the way you moved to me, gradually but intently until you stood by me to ask: *'What's your name?*

BOOK 4

SOMETHING INTELLIGENT
HAPPENING IN THE DARK

The excitement which your movement stirred, increased thrillingly in intensity with every movement of yours. Something intelligent was happening. Happening in the dark. Something I could not explain. It was happening inside of me. Spreading a wave of warmth to play across my surface with shadows and light coming out to play. Engaged in full, I wondered if it would be as it was becoming.

You wanted to know me. You wanted to understand me. *What's your name?* I heard again and again. You studied me intently before asking me my name. You have been deep in thought as though I matter, as though I am important. You were struck and you followed in stride. You were drawn and you drew to know. I perceived a searching spirit within you. You have been wondering visibly as though something called you and you are wondering what it was. You seem to be engaged by what you see and you seem possessed by many thoughts. You appear to be thinking: 'There is more to it', 'What is its name, the name I cannot see'.

What's your name? I heard again. 'What's your name' became your quest. We both have this quest in common, I thought. The

11

quest to know the unknown. I am interested in knowing me. You are interested in knowing my name. I need a journey to find me. You need to be part of the journey to find the name. A mutually beneficial alliance of interest appeared to be formed from the formless. An attraction to the unknown. The form of that unknown remains unknown.

Excitement welled up in me and enthusiastically I asked: *Would you really come with me? Would you really be my companion? All the way? Through the journey?* It was then you told me what I did not know. You told me that when I thought these thoughts:

"What's in a name?'
'Am I in a name?
Is a name in me?"

You thought the following thoughts:

"Who am I?
Are you in my name?
Is my name in you?"

You told me that when I thought these thoughts:

"A name could be anything, everything or nothing at all"

You thought these thoughts:

"Is a name everything?
Is everything in a name?
Is a name nothing at all?
Is nothing a name at all?"

You told me that you have been wondering whether it was I who caught your eye when you saw me from a distance or whether it was you who caught sight of me when I saw you from a distance. Whether it was my thoughts which called you or whether it was you who attracted my thoughts? Whether I was drawn to you or whether it was you who was drawn to me? Was it you who was struck by the way I looked, the way I looked at you, beyond the surface boring deep within? Was it I who stirred and steered towards you? Was it me who began to move, gradually but intently towards you, until you heard me ask: '*What's your name?*

BOOK 5

MOVE TO NAME

Name. What a thought. It's now all about name. Name a name. Name any name. A name can be anything, everything or nothing at all. A name is a form. A form of address. An expression. Expression of thought. Thought in human mind. Expressed in human words. Made in human term. The term in human mind. Formless in thought. Made to form. Named as formed. Formed is made. Made is formed. What's in a name? Am I in a name? Is a name in me? What's your name? The name in your mind. You bear name in mind. Are you bearing mine? Are you bearing my name? Is my name in you? Are you in my name?

Who am I? Did I think that? Was it your own thought?

You have been looking at me yet not seeing my name? You are occupied by the thought of my name. You want to know more. You want to understand more. What you already know is not enough. Being here at this time, looking at me from where you are is not opening you up to the knowledge you seek.

You want to know more but your present viewing point does not deliver the name you seek. Maybe a move will move you to the name. Would you move to the unknown with me? The unknown where the unknown is known.

If you come with me, both of us can find me. When I find me, I would then make a name. A name which conveys all. A name which tells tales. Tales about me. And you will get to know the name. The name which you seek. The name which I will make. Just as I want to be known. In the name I want to be called.

Maybe another space may have what this space does not have and reveal what this space has not revealed. Should we explore another space? I will tell you about a space in the next space.

BOOK 6

ON THE WALL

You see, for a very long time, I was just hanging there. They came and went, peered into me and spoke.

I was hanging on the wall.

That was how I lived. From one light to another, from one dark to another. But every dark was unique. Every dark has its light. Every light has its dark. Then came this one dark which revealed this light. It is in that dark that it is now happening. The stir which steered is the steer which stirred. It does not make sense to you.

Of course, you don't understand. How can you? How can anyone? You were not at the beginning. The beginning remains unknown, even now is still unknown. You were not there when it happened and could not testify that it happened. You did not experience that which could have informed so you remain uninformed.

Before now remains a mystery, even now is a mystery. The present and the past are both mysteries which is why you want to know more. '*My mother is just like that*', definitely tells much more. It is in the future but also in the present and in the past depending on your starting point. To you, it may still be unknown, even though it is here with us, right under us, in this very space, in the presence of now, in our own very present.

If you choose to find '*My mother is just like that*', and get to

16

know its unknown, its unknown may help you to know much more. It's somewhere around here, if you choose to search.

If you find it, you will find me there. The path is not always straight forward. Sometimes, it may confuse, sometimes it may be unseen, so take this beam with you. It is a constant companion and will always show you the way. But the choice is always yours. Whether to stir and steer in accordance with its direction, whether to accept its companionship, whether to totally ignore its existence.

BOOK 7

WILL YOU COME WITH ME?

Remember I told you in **BOOK 'MOVE TO THE NAME'** that I will tell you about a space? I have now told you about that space. That space is **BOOK 'ON THE WALL'**. I have kept my promise. With the information you now have, you are free to do what you are moved to do. The choice is always yours. To be with me now that you know more about me or not to be with me. To be yourself or to be others. To be with a few or in a crowd. To think for yourself or to follow the rest. At a cross-road, the choice is always yours, whether to go back the way you came or to explore other ways.

At this juncture, you are free to choose, whether to find out more from other spaces, whether to continue on this path, whether to go a separate way, whether to walk this path alone or whether to be with me.

On this path and on my part, I still want you to be my partner. I still want you to be my companion. I am still attracted to your thoughts. I still want both of us to share the experience of discovering the mystery of the unknown. Will you be with me? Will you come with me?

BOOK 8

THE JOURNEY OF YOU AND ME

As you are still wondering how you got here, I will tell you what I know. At the outset, you caught my eye. I saw you in the distance and you struck me. I do not know how you came to be at the point where our eyes were caught. But the way you looked at me captivated me. Your thoughts then attracted me and I became drawn to you. It was at that point that you began to move. Gradually towards me, until you stood by me and asked: '*What's your name?*

Stirring many thoughts in me is that question '*What's your name*'. Come to think of it. What's really in a name? Am I in a name? Is a name in me? A name can be anything, anything can be a name. A name can be everything, everything can be a name. A name can be nothing at all, nothing at all can be a name.

You are wondering how you got here. I am wondering as well. Many things about me remain unknown to me. Many things are being revealed to me by encounters and strikes. You struck me. Strikes set off reactions. Encounters become discoveries. Adventures draw out names and make known the unknown. As to that question '*What's your name*', I have not yet made a name, so I cannot tell a name. I get to share a name only when I've made a name. Where I come from, you see, we make our names ourselves. So this is the reason I appeared. This is why I am here. I'm here to

19

make a name but have not quite made it. I want to create a special, a unique sort of name bearing everything I am. For me to create such name, I must first create myself, adding everything I want in a name. Will you come with me on this adventure? The adventure to make myself. The adventure to know myself. A journey of you and me.

Now you know what I know, do you still want to know more? Will you come with me to find my name? Do you still want to know my name?

BOOK 9

MAKE A NAME

I am deeply pleased that you decided to come with me. You chose to be with me. Whilst on this journey, you may call me what you choose. You may call me any name. Many names may come to mind. You may call me any of them, some of them or all of them. You may call me what you like, what grabs you and what you grasp. Your choice is unlimited. As unlimited as your feelings. You may call me any name which captures how I make you feel at every stage of our journey. Feelings change so names will change according to the changing feelings. Make a name to go with the feeling. Make that name your companion. Call that name for as long as it remains unchanged. When it changes to another name, make another name. A new name becomes your new companion. An old name presents you with a choice - keep or discard.

You are free to make any name. You are free to call me whatever you make. You are free to make any name your companion. But the name I make is the only name I want to be known by. But I will be entertained by what you make of me and the names you choose to call me.

When I find myself, I will make a name. A name which conveys me. That me which my adventures found. A name which delivers me. Everything about me. A name which captures my spirit. The spirits my adventures stirred and woke, invoked and called. A name which captivates thoughts and activates spirits. A name which engages and connects spirits. Spirits stirred and steered in my name. A name which I will see come alive in me, which rises above me and towers beyond me, which becomes me, brought out by my adventures and my relationship with others. A name well prepared and well brewed, so well made and so well created just as we do where I come from. A name of my own making and of my own choosing. A name which is my pride and joy.

I will proudly call out that name in the dark. I will invoke it with a dance. I will receive its spirit in glory. I will entertain it with honour and ceremony, splendour and dignity, grandeur and privilege. I will call it out when it is ready and it will echo in you and spread out for all to see and you will be able to see me in all my ramifications and manifestations in that name of my own making. That name I made so well.

That name remains in the dark, that dark of beauty where beauty resides until it is called out. That dark of beauty from where expressions of beauty emanate. The name I will make will express beauty. The name I will make will emanate from beauty. A towering form of beauty emitting beauty in form and in formless. That name remains unknown and I will journey to the unknown for as long as it remains unknown.

The unknown has no form because it is unknown. Formless is its form because its form is formless. The formless may shed its 'less' in order to be identified as form but its 'less' is not less and is not lessened. Rather its 'less' continues to be more as it expands active though remaining unknown in the abode of the known.

When the known meets the unknown, the meeting becomes an experience. An experience of forms and the formless. An experience of the known and the unknown. An experience of the shaped and the shapeless. In that encounter, the unknown may become known and the known may become unknown. When it becomes known it takes shape and form, and soars high in the abode of the known. The unknown presented in a form to shape the known. The known present in unknown to form the formless.

The name I will make remains unknown. The name I will make remains formless. The name I will make remains shapeless. The name I will make continues to reside in that dark of beauty where beauty resides until it is called out. I am deeply pleased that you chose to be with me. Make a name for yourself. I am making mine.

BOOK 10

BEAMING COMPANION

In the other space, the space called **'ON THE WALL'**, I told you to take a beam with you. A beam which is a constant companion in the journey to the unknown. You did not understand what I meant so now I shade more dark on it.

'LOVE TO YOU ALWAYS, LOVE TO ALL ALWAYS' is what I call a beam. A beaming companion. Whilst your feelings are changing and your names are changing, your beaming companion never changes. It remains your constant companion throughout the journey to the unknown whether you know it or not, whether you are on this part or on another path. It always helps you find your way whenever you remember to look through its beam. The intelligence is in the dark. The colourless intelligence in the dark. If it is colourless and in the dark, it is sometimes not seen unless you have the right glasses, spectacle and magnifier. Do look out for it whenever you feel lost and need a direction. It may appear like this:

LOVE TO YOU ALWAYS
LOVE TO ALL ALWAYS

BOOK 11

MY MOTHER IS JUST LIKE THAT

My creator calls me 'Sunflowers on the terrace'
The name my creator made
I call my creator 'dad'
The name another made
My mum calls dad 'Gorgeous'
Mum really thinks dad is
My mother is just like that

If mum is in this space
She'll call you a sun
A star, a demi-God
A planet, names like that
She means it, for sure
My mother is just like that

My mum's a story teller
She tells me that the sun
Shines light all the time
Even when we don't see it
Likewise, humans can beam LOVE
Seen and unseen
That every human pore can be a pour of LOVE

That every glistening sweat can be radiating LOVE
Emitting glow of LOVE
From every single cell
And every strand of hair

This made me ask my mum
What is LOVE?
The answer I got from mum is an encyclopaedia of LOVE
Which starts just like this:
LOVE is ENERGY
The ENERGY which generates INTELLIGENCE
The INTELLIGENCE which generates beauty
The beauty in different forms, but also in no form
LOVE is the unseen energy which can appear to be seen,
touched and perceived with all senses
LOVE exists even when unseen and may not be touched or
perceived at all even when it is the surrounding which is
surrounding
Mum then told me that LOVE does not fit into human-
worded definition because it is beyond human words
LOVE is that formless which can take any form
A state of being, a condition, the profound, the overwhelm-
ing
LOVE is the energy which forms intelligence
It is the intelligence in the form of energy
It is the energy in the form of intelligence
The intelligence which energises and induces creativity in
all things
The intelligence which liberates and creates diverse beauty
The intelligence which produces uniqueness
And harmonises all random, all order and all uniqueness
The energy and intelligence which heals and soothes
That's my mum for you

My mother is just like that

Mum said that LOVE induces the aura and aroma of beauty
In which all diversity thrives
And in which all creativity flourishes
Stirring spirits to euphoria
Nurturing and nourishing human mind to be endlessly beautiful
Stirring humans and other beings to create more and more beauty
Endlessly in diverse LOVE-forms and formless which themselves continuously unfold and multiply
Mum said that when a human mind is filled with LOVE you will know
Mum said that all around the human mind will perceive the LOVE overflowing from the human mind
The overflow is perceived as openness, transparency, peace of mind, understanding, healing gestures including kindness and actions which harmonise uniqueness and beauty, and plant unity and peace
That's what mum said
My mother is just like that

Mum told me that LOVE steers beings into its state
Its state is the State of LOVE
Where LOVE rains and reigns supreme
The supreme reign rains LOVE-rays, LOVE-radiance, LOVE-shine
LOVE induces its aura, stirring excitement to thrill
LOVE induces minds to expand beyond walls into places of beauty
And induces beings to expand into the nothingness which is LOVE

That's what mum said
My mother is just like that

Then this thought came to me
*'LOVE sounds just like a combination of air, sun, fertile
soil and water'.*
Mum must have heard my thought because she said this to
me
It is true that LOVE gives life so air is like LOVE
It is true that LOVE radiates and spans centuries so the sun
is like LOVE
It is true that LOVE rehydrates and refreshes so water is
like LOVE
It is true that LOVE supports and nourishes so fertile soil is
like LOVE
You are right to see LOVE as a combination of all those
things rather than just one of those
You are right to see LOVE as bigger and more expanse
than the air, the sun, the water, the fertile soil
Every air which sustains life has LOVE within it
LOVE sustains spirits of things and sustains life on earth
LOVE is timeless and boundless
LOVE-rays reach and move millions to expand
Billowing and unfolding inexhaustibly in LOVE
Sun travels in light years
But LOVE radiates in LOVE which is not measured in
years or in time
Particles of LOVE are in sun and sun is in LOVE
In LOVE with all it touches
LOVE nourishes all and does not burn, so humans need no
LOVE-screen
There is LOVE in water and water is in LOVE
In LOVE with all it sustains, rehydrates and sustains

LOVE is a life-saver, life-maker, ice-breaker, nurturing
vapour, fountain of life, life's jacket, boat and coat
Beings could drown and die in water, but in LOVE beings
live even when submerged in LOVE forever
LOVE nourishes with beauty, all beings planted in it
Unlike fertile soil, LOVE does not change in flood, or in
rain or in the sun
LOVE solidly supports, builds and lifts
Unlike solid land, LOVE's support is not eroded by flood
and not turned into a desert by scorching sun
That's what mum said
My mother is just like that

Mum writes LOVE in capital letters because she thinks it is
supreme
The supreme state of being, the supreme state of LOVE
The being and the state, the form and the formless
Expanding and boundless
Unlimited and ageless
Timeless and wireless
That's mum for you
My mother is just like that

I LOVE my mum and dad but we follow what we like
I LOVE and follow sun
Mum LOVES and follows LOVE
Dad follows the unknown
The unknown I do not know

Because I follow sun
Some call me sun-follower, sunflower or names like that
 Because Mum follows LOVE
Some call mum LOVE-follower, LOVEbearer, LOVEbeing

As Dad follows Unknown
Some call dad what they do not know

Though I do not see my dad, I know that dad's in me
My dad is not just one
All of them are dad
In a way I'm the dad
Because many are seen in one
The uncountable one is also one

All my dads are dad
Dad does not mean a male
Dad is just a name
Just as mum is a name
Mum does not mean female
Dad and mum are just names
Of all that is in me
The seen and the unseen
That made me what I am

I think I'm in my dad
Or was some time ago
For dad made me so well
From nothing and from things
The nothing some call thoughts
The things you touch and see
The body is the form, the seen and the thing
The unseen is the thought
The spirit in thought
The formless made to form

My mum is quite unique
She says, you're made unique

That no one will find you anywhere else in the world
She means 'another you'
Exactly as you are, anywhere else in the world
She says you're the only one ever made as you are
But versions of yourself can be seen in thoughts and in memory
Versions which you created by what you say or do
Versions which are planted through encounters of all kinds

Mum says you're made special so as to exhibit and share your own very Younique
Then she told me of the bee and something called pollen
And how by being itself, the bee spreads the pollen
I did not understand
So I said 'mum please explain'
Mum confused me the more when her reply came as this:
'YOU' means YOUnique', unique as some call it
That's my mum for you
My mother is just like that

My mum can make you think whether or not you like to think
My mum can make you think when you do not want to think
I did not want to think about YOU or YOUnique
But the thought has been planted and the thinking just began
"YOUnique means YOU
YOU means YOUnique?"
What does she mean by that?

Then it dawned on me
Just as an idea of me was planted inside dad's thoughts

Just as dad's visions and spirit stirred and inspired dad to
create me to be seen
I can create and plant beauties inside minds and memories
By just being myself
By just being like the bee

Everything in me combines to make me what I am.
Some parts of me are seen
Some parts of me unseen
Even parts which are seen, contain things unseen
Products, reactions and combinations which have changed
state
Are mixed up in me and no longer seen as separate entities
Products made by known and by some unknown
Make me a creation by many
That many in one
A product of many lovers
The uncountable one made by the entire
A product of PROFOUND

It dawned on me just then
That I am that formless
Made into a form
But my form can become
Formless in minds or forms in thoughts and in memory

By just being myself, the form of myself
By just being a form, myself in my form
My formless can beam beauty
My beam can create beauties
Beauty in minds, beauty in memory
A projection of me into mind and space
A projection of beauty, a beam of LOVE

As only I can beam
As only I can form
As only I can create
By just being me
A transmission of me, in the frequency of now
If I transmit beauty, I become a channel of beauty

Shining my YOUnique is like shining like the sun
Being my own self is like pollen and the bee
My mum once told me that the sun shines so well
Even when nothing is applauding its awe
It shines not to impress
Though its impression is left
Wherever it touches
It shines all the time
Even when we do not see it
It shines so well
It shines for its own self

Sun occupies itself
By spreading its light full-time
Its profession, its occupation
Its full-time job, its only vocation
Is to shine shine shine
As only it can shine
Its rays reach to touch
Its warmth can make beauty
To sprout, to grow, to be
In being itself, others get to be themselves
And bask in its warmth, to be what they can be
Whatever is on sun's path, gets to be touched
Unless sun-blocks are in the way

That's what mum said
My mother is just like that

That made me think
Indeed I'm like the sun
In me is everything I need to be myself
To radiate full-time, to shine all the time
And to enjoy shining well, even without applause
Around me, beings of different forms are stirring their unique just like the sun
And I can connect to the beauty in all the beings around me
The seen and unseen, and be stirred to radiate and expand formlessly
To continue creating myself and be the best me I can be
My formless expansion can touch everything on my path
Unless expansion-block has been placed on the path
To block connection or divert attention

Just like the sun, my radiance may shine away some beings
And attract other beings
When some beings peer into my radiance
From an angle of misunderstanding, my radiance may dazzle
Causing a kind of blindness
My intense LOVE energy may shine away the destructive
And refine the raw in me making it LOVE-refined and polished

My mum enjoys being unique
She calls it being herself
Just like a bee is being itself
The bee infects the world with its own unique beauty
By merely being itself

The sun infects the world with own unique beauty
By merely being itself
I'd like to infect my world with my own unique beauty
By being the best me I can be
Beaming myself and enjoying the beam
Creating beauty and variety

I do understand my mum
YOU means YOUnique
And YOUnique means I am unique
I can be the best version of me
That me which I can create
By connecting to all the beauty around me
With the connection of the beauty within me
That within which beams beauty into minds
Projected in the frequency of now
And when I beam myself
Any mind which encounters a version of me
Will bear that version of me as the image of me
Just as the sun leaves its impression wherever it touches
So the beamed version of me imprints itself
Wherever my impression is left

Mum's language of YOUnique
Which was once unknown to me
I have now come to know
When mum's YOUnique shines through
It becomes a transmitter, a transformer, a reflection
Reaching, transforming, infecting and reflecting all who
connect with it

My mum's reflections, quite good an infection
When mum's YOUniqueness beams through

It impresses beauty in minds and memory
It inspires thoughts and conversations too
Like bee on pollen, infecting the pollen world by merely
being itself
Mum pollinates her own world with her own words of
LOVE
Like the sun by being itself sprays rays of warmth which
infect the world with beauty
Mum sprays her seeds of LOVE and impregnates minds
with thoughts of LOVE
My mother just makes you think
So that you may come to know
That's my mum for you
My mother is just like that

I LOVE my mum so much
My mum, the tales she tells
I know she tells the 'truth'
In her own way that is
Understanding YOUnique
Got me quite excited
And all sorts of thoughts
Appeared to possess
The thought which possessed most
Is the thought I'd like to tell

The thought that I'd like to tell my own tales appeared and
possessed me
I'd like to express my own views
And even write a book
A book of adventures
Yes, I heard myself echo
I'd like to go on journeys

I'd like to tell my tales

But what shall I call my book?
This thought entertained me
It thrilled me to no end
What shall I name the book?
The idea of a name
A name can be anything, everything or nothing at all
Should I use the name dad made?
The name dad calls me?
Then I started to think….
"ADVENTURES OF SUNFLOWERS ON THE TERRACE"

Then it dawned on me
And I sighed with regret
It is impossible
This dream of adventure
Adventures are the privilege of those with legs
I am only a painting
Hanging on the wall
My place is on the wall

"How can I write a book of journeys, views and adventures when I'm hanging on this wall?" This thought possessed me but also depressed me.

Then I remembered that mum once said:
When an idea grows inside of your LOVE
You will LOVE the idea so much
You will dream and think of the idea all the time
You will even begin to live the idea
But the idea does not leave you

It comes alive in you
It comes to live in you
It expands and grows
And becomes your constant companion, your obsession,
your life
My mother is just like that
Her thoughts are just like that

But come to think of it
My idea of a book
My book of adventures
I think and dream of it
So much and all the time
"But how can I write a book?
A book of adventures?
When my space remains the wall?
The writing on the wall?"
Those thoughts detained me
And troubled me so much
My mother came to mind and I remembered some words
my mum once said
If an idea plants itself
Right inside of your LOVE
There isn't very much
You can do about it
It will beat every bit of heart
And liven every breath of life
Get you pregnant with ideas
Make you deliver the idea

When an idea grows inside of your LOVE
You LOVE the idea so much
So much to dream and think

Of the idea all the time
You even live the idea
But the idea does not leave you
The idea comes to life
To be your companion
My mother is just like that
My mum just talks like that

The thought excited me
And even entertained me
And replayed itself
Over and over in versions
Mum said there are ideas
Which actually choose you
And when they do strike you
They'll leave you with one choice
To do just as they bid
They will make you do things
You thought you could never do
They will make you conceive
In order to give birth
The baby is the idea
Appearing to be seen
In a form which it chose

Mum said some ideas
Fall on fertile soil
And grow and give birth
To even more ideas
She said some other ideas
May fall on minds
Not so fertile
And live just for a little

She said ideas spring up
Sometimes from nothingness
And are the formless
Which can take form
Some exhibit themselves
But before they can take root
Other ideas grow and block them
Blocking their view and root
Blocking route to sustenance
So they wither or stop growing
Or even die a kind of death

Mum said that when ideas choose you
They have their own reason
For choosing you and not me
You may wonder 'why me'
And think you do not have legs
Or that you are not good enough
She said the ideas which choose you
Are those ideas which plant themselves deep and secure
inside of your LOVE
And fill you with overflowing passion
And thrill you to no end
My mum is just like that
She always thinks like that
Her thoughts sometimes confuse
But that's my mum for you
My mother is just like that

But come to think of it
My idea of a book
My book of adventures
I think and dream of it

So much and all the time
So is it my idea?
Or am I chosen by the idea?
Is my form the form of an idea?
Or am I forming this idea?
Am I writing the book of adventure or is the book of
adventure writing me?

But how can I write a book, a book of adventures, when my space
remains the wall? The writing on the wall?

Those thoughts came to me

And troubled me so much
But were replaced again
By the replaying thought
If an idea plants itself right inside of your LOVE
There isn't very much
You can do about it
It will beat every bit of heart
And liven every breath of life
Gets you pregnant with idea
Makes you deliver the idea

I kept thinking of my adventure
I kept beaming in the thoughts of adventure
Then this happened!
It really did happen!
I did not know that this can happen!
That if I think it long enough, I become what I think!
I saw myself leaving the wall
Well I thought I saw myself
Indeed I felt myself leaving the wall

I felt myself going on adventure
I'm sure it was my mum who took me down that day
From my place on the wall to tour places of the world
I became excited, very excited
That was a singular achievement
Planting my dream inside mum's dream
Yes, I planted my own dream right inside my mum's dream
Mum thought it was her dream, when one day I left my wall
to start to tour the world
Mum thought it was her dream to take me on a tour of the
world
But it was my own dream planted right inside of her LOVE

But what I'm not so sure is…
Am I in idea or is idea in me?
Is an idea inside my LOVE?
Or is my LOVE inside an idea?
Am I pregnant with the idea?
Or is the idea pregnant with me?
Is a dream an idea or is idea a dream?
Is it all a dream?
If so whose dream is it?

Those thoughts possessed me
And even startled me when thoughts began to unfold
And I began to observe
The vision of myself
The vision I gave myself
The vision myself gave me
The vision of here and now

I have reached here
I am now here with you

I turn to ask myself
What was all that about?
What is here to see?
You, is what I see
Right here now we meet
Thanks for being here
Come let's continue this journey
Let's visit the unknown

You ask for rules of engagement
I will tell you this
There are no hard and fast rules
This is only an adventure
Please treat it as such
You always have your thoughts
And the choice is yours
I will share my own thoughts
I will even think aloud
My thoughts are not always clear
And sometimes full of mistakes
And imperfections too
Sometimes regular
And sometimes irregular
Sometimes logical
And sometimes illogical
But that is the nature of thoughts
If you are a bit confused
Don't worry too much about it
Just know that it is a normal state
In this plane of understanding and misunderstanding,
known and unknown

This is only an adventure

LOVE is our only guide
Please follow LOVE's instruction
LOVE is LOVE
You will know LOVE
When you experience the state of LOVE
The LOVE within us
Is our supreme and ultimate leader
And we can always connect
To it to connect to all
We always have a choice
To share or not to share our thoughts or our all
When we share thoughts, it is to enrich and not to destroy
We are uniquely crafted but we have LOVE in common
We may think alike or differ in thoughts
As you have chosen to be on this journey with me
May I suggest that we choose to share our thoughts even
when it is most difficult for us to share our thoughts
To share our thoughts is to communicate for the purpose of
understanding each other better
To build a bridge of understanding which becomes a bridge
of LOVE
To revere and nurture each other's uniqueness
Instead of engaging in heated destructive arguments

I know that it is easier to avoid discussing sensitive subjects
including religious ones

But may I propose that we learn to discuss them even if it
involves going through the 'heat of the moment' in order to get to
the 'LOVE of always' which is the uniting passion at the core of
all things

May I propose that we work as a team to kill the discrimination
and not the communication, to resurrect the communication and
bury the discrimination which harms and destroys humans and

others

If we work from the state of LOVE, we will be subject to the RULE OF LOVE over and above the rule of law

We will work as a team playing towards the same goal of removing from power, destruction, hate, abuse, maltreatment, oppression, slavery of all kinds, violence, malice, suspicions and fear and enthrone LOVE to lead in all things, we will share the intelligence of LOVE in thoughts on all subjects knowing that we are learning about LOVE not manipulating to overpower and dominate

If we work from the state of LOVE, sensitive subjects will not divide us

I will now share my thoughts and hope you share yours too

When you cannot read my thoughts, know I'm reading your thoughts

Thanks again for coming along on this journey
Your companionship is already making a positive difference in my world
Bear this in mind, please bear this in mind
It is a privilege to be on this journey
The journey of adventures
The privilege of the legged
The privilege is the fact of being here
Being present, here and now
I will like to know myself
And find out how dad looks
And all you and I have in common
And meet the uniqueness in everyone
I am really pleased to meet you
Here is a great place
And on this journey of adventures I submit ONLY to the RULE OF LOVE

And the leadership of LOVE

What should I call you? You ask
'It depends', I reply, on how I make you feel
What state are you in now you're journeying with me?
State of LOVE or state of hate?
State of wonder, awe or joy?
Full of smiles or full of frown?
State of peace or state of stress?
Just make a name from that state
That state you find yourself when you are with me
What does my presence stir in you?
What are you steered to do?
Create a name from that
And you will have procreated a name
This is an opportunity
An opportunity of a lifetime
An opportunity to procreate
An opportunity to be creative
An opportunity to reproduce
A name can be anything, everything or nothing at all
So create yourself a name for me
You will then be a creator of a name
My creator created a name

You may find this difficult to believe. I certainly will find it difficult to believe if I am you. I do not know how my creator looks though I have seen works of creation. They all come out with different looks. So I do not know if they look like my creator or if I look like my creator because I do not know how my creator looks.

'The being you call your mother, how do you know she is your mother?' is the question you ask me. You are right to ask me that question. Given that I say that mother and father are in me, how can I know my mother and say that I have never seen my father?

To know is not the same thing as to see. It is true that I have not seen my father but I know my mother very well. You ask me how I know she is my mother when I do not know how my father looks. You are right to suggest that the being I call my mother might as well be my father. I know she is my mother because I am with her all the time. She is always with me and takes me out from time to time, and together we exercise different minds in different spaces. She looks after me, nurtures me and nourishes me. She is in my thoughts. She is my thoughts. That's how I know she is my mother. But you are right. She might also be my father. Father and Mother, dad and mum are only names. What is in a name? A name can be anything, everything or nothing at all.

Look over there my dear friend! Can you see what I am seeing? Look again. Something is emerging in the distance. I want to know what it is. Let's go my dear friend. Let's visit that unknown.

BOOK 12

GUARANTEED TO THRILL

Look over there!
Do you see what I see emerging?
The river over there
Weaving through its cursive words
The flowers chanting songs
The mountains writing sound
Is that a bird I see?
I cannot make them out
They seem so far away but I'd like to get to them
I'm in awe my dear friend
Hurry let's get to them…

THE EXHIBITION OF A LIFETIME

GUARANTEED TO THRILL

ADMISSION IS FREE

TAKE OFF YOUR COVERINGS

It's becoming clearer as we draw closer. I hope you saw it…

"THE EXHIBITION OF A LIFETIME. GUARANTEED TO THRILL. ADMISSION IS FREE".

We are thrill seekers. We followed the call. A chance to be thrilled. You and I are here. Here to experience. To experience a thrill. Guaranteed to thrill, we are ready to be thrilled. Is it just me or is the light in this space beginning to dim? It's as if we triggered a move by entering this space. The space has now become as dark as void can be. Is that a voice coming from nowhere? A voice rising in the dark?

"Welcome to this experience. Admission is free but the gate does not open until you remove all coverings including all footwear, undergarments, socks and tights. You will not be needing them here and they may not be in fashion when you leave. They may no longer fit at the time of exit. So please know for sure, that you will never see your coverings ever again if you choose to remove them in order to visit what you do not know"

This is very awkward but out of curiosity and for the promise of a thrill, the coverings must go, so I said to myself. All of it, every single one. We found ourselves bare, with no covering at all. The voice continued.

"If you feel exposed, uncomfortable and vulnerable from taking off your coverings, please put this on. Though you cannot see what I am giving to you, it covers all. It keeps you warm in the cold and cool in the heat. It is the most precious covering any being could don. It is always in fashion, always expanding in dimensions, always moulding and beautifying all. If you choose to wear it, you need only reach out to touch and you will find it even

49

in pitch darkness. You will be thrilled and entertained as you learn how to wear it. You wear it well when you allow its flow to become your own special fashion statement. Your own individual style.

Of course, you always have a choice. You can choose to stay still in this void or choose to move. If you choose to move, please know that you cannot move back even if you feel yourself going back. It may be because there is no back. It may be because you do not know where you came from. It may be because you have forgotten the way back. It may be because that gate which opened to let you through can only open once for you and does not open to let any who has passed through it to go back into it. It may be because there is nowhere you came from other than where you are. It may be because this void is all there is and there is nothing like the route you thought you came from.

If you choose to move, you may also choose to make the best of this void, engaging with all that unfolds. If you choose to stay still, you may stare in the void and lament about the lost route. The choice is yours, to either make a move or to stay still as you are, where you are. "

The voice gradually faded leaving silence to reign. The awe of stillness struck. It was moving and moved us to remain still. The silence commanded reverence and we bowed in spirit. The atmosphere was charged. Charged in silence, the beauty of stillness. It was peaceful. It was soothing. It was enriching and we wanted nothing else as we absorbed this beauty and merged with stillness. Time passed but did not seem like it passed. We were content and fulfilled. It felt somehow sacrilegious to disturb the aura of stillness with any sort of movement. There was no need to even move our eyes. No difference between our eyes being closed and our eyes being open. The sight was the same closed or open. Our sight was darkness, our vision was silent. No path came to us. The path which brought us no longer spoke to us. We did not know which way was backward or which way was sideways, which way was forward, upward or downward. We remained still. The silence was sacred. We chose to absorb the moment. At that moment, a thought appeared: "GUARANTEED TO THRILL". It stirred excitement. It brought back the thought of our journey. Remembering that we are beings without coverings, we reached out in unison for a new covering. Reaching out for the new covering appeared to trigger a move of some unknown. The aura of stillness was in harmony with the move. As we moved to touch, the reign of stillness moved to welcome some movements playing out in the distance. We were captivated by something unfolding in the void, gradually coming through from the distance. It is a dark. A cloud of black. A kind of light. It continued to emerge and gradually revealed itself in this form:

THE SONG OF MY BREATH
This song I sing is known to everyone
Like a bird sings its own tune, so I sing mine
Not because it's original but because it's my origin
The song of LOVE is the song of my breath
LOVE TO YOU ALWAYS
LOVE TO ALL ALWAYS

Before I could make a connection to follow this line of thought, something extraordinary distracted me. I noticed a development unravelling in the distance. So I did not have time to follow my line of thought as another line was appearing and forming in the distance.

What's that in the distance? I thought. Are you perceiving as I am? I asked. Look look look over there but it is coming closer to us! Can you see that parade? Before my eyes, here and now. The dark. A kind of black. The black. A kind of light. It is coming closer. One by one it is converging and aligning. A kind of parade. You must be seeing it now as I am seeing it. Can you see each dark arrive with its different kind of illumination? The void seems to be enjoying accommodating all these different darks and lights. By accommodating all of the appearances, the void itself is becoming transformed. Each of the dark is kind of light and each of the light is a kind of dark. They appear and become something in a line. So I will call each dark a being, a kind of beam.

The being first appears as infinitesimal dark in light. A dot travelling to the plane, at first not clear, not known, not understood but gradually emerging more meaningful. The dot continues unfolding in the void, breaking through to appear.

So you are not seeing it from the same point of view. I am only sharing how I am perceiving it. When you are ready to share your own thoughts, I will listen to your thoughts.

Look over there my dear friend! How can you not be seeing what I am seeing? More beings lining up. Not just first one but many are here. They have come to stay but for how long I do not know. This is thrilling! Look at that captivating line-up of black on white! Appearing one after the other. Are you seeing them as I am seeing them? They are lining up and increasing in number. Come look from my point of view. This is what is lining up. This is what I'm seeing and how I'm seeing…

BOOK 13
CONTENTS

WHAT ARE WE?

We are not poems
             We are just thoughts
             Raw as we are
Conceived unseen
             Random in nature
Just as we are

Nothing but thoughts
             Thoughts of LOVE
LOVE in capital
             Not in lower case
Repetitive sometimes
             But it has to be
Of course it needs to be
             There's never an overdose
Of LOVE LOVE LOVE
             LOVE and never stop

We were the unseen
             Which you now see
We follow no rules
             Except ones in thoughts
And ones in ideas
             Of LOVE LOVE LOVE
Of LOVE and never stop

We are just here
             To start a conversation
To bridge not to split
             To communicate not to offend
Exploring the concept

Of LOVE in capital
Not in lower case
LOVE TO YOU ALWAYS
LOVE TO ALL ALWAYS
The message we bear

WHAT I THOUGHT AT THIS POINT

My dear friend, are you what I am? Are you excited? Visiting this unknown. The journey of two books is the journey of here and now. The journey of here and now is the journey of these books. Not of tomorrow and the next, not of yesterday or the then but of now and herein. The journey of two books. Journeying the present. Exploring here and now. To know the here and now. One present at a time. I'm so excited. To be here and now. And to have met CONTENTS

And all it has. LOVE TO YOU ALWAYS. LOVE TO ALL ALWAYS. The beam and companion.

I met here and now.

BOOK 14
THE BOOK OF THE
BREATHING SPACE

Waow!
What a thrilling space
What a great show!
Guaranteed to thrill!
And we were thrilled
Look over there my dear friend
Is that the bird we saw from the other space?
It seems to be speaking to us
Come my dear friend, let's get closer

I am popularly known as the bird. I am standing on a headstone which is not set in stone. May I welcome you to my world, the world of conversation, a space where ideas interact and where you can conceive yourself a new. In this world of ideas every being is an exhibit on exhibition, the exhibition of beings. In the world of conversation, things are a little different which is why I stand on a headstone to tell the tale. In this world of communication, every being is a writing which other beings can read as you are reading me and as I am reading you. Not every communication will make sense, not every being will understand what you understand and you will not always understand what others understand. Some are written in a language that is beyond understanding. Some are written in such a way that it is so difficult to follow. Some are difficult to begin with, but repeated reading makes them easier to understand. Some, you certainly need a dictionary to read. Many look simple on the outside but hard on the inside. Patience is key to understanding some writings. In this space, you are a writing, communicating in different forms. Every writing in this space is a writer and can write more, or erase or change some writings already written on own headstone. Each being is a headstone on which compositions appear. You can return to the headstone as often you want to erase and add as you change and move. By standing on a headstone, I have become part of the headstone, the headstone bearing me.

The unknown you are about to enter is a special space. You will meet all sorts. First the unwanted child, followed by the wanted child. From among all sorts, choose the child you want to wear. Wear it for your tour of this unknown. Entering this plane makes you a child of this plane. We would meet again. At the LOVERS' gate.

LOVE TO YOU ALWAYS
LOVE TO ALL ALWAYS

THE SPACE YOU ARE ABOUT TO ENTER IS A SACRED SPACE

1 THE UNWANTED CHILD

In the beginning was me
I looked around and chose my mum
Then drove my father to it
The battle ensued
My mother resisted me and tried to remove me
I stayed on fast and almost lost out

I am the unwanted child who survived to live
I bear my mark, the mark of strength
I'm older than my mum and older than my dad
I chose them both, they did not choose me
I will keep them both for they survived me

You ask about the fathers
One father was indifferent
The other did not know
Another wanted it when mum didn't want
Another didn't want but mum did want
I wanted to breathe
In that breathing space
I chose my mum
And drove dad to it

Do you want to be me and see things through my eyes?
You can for this journey
Wear me if you choose
Make me your headstone
The choice is yours
To be me or not to be
And know what I know

Here I am
The unwanted child
LOVE TO YOU ALWAYS
LOVE TO ALL ALWAYS

2   THE WANTED CHILD

In the beginning was me
I was looking around when I heard the voice calling for a
child, a child to love
The mind was made up, fertile was the womb
The heart beating fast, the longing unceasing
Others ignored the call saying she's not fat enough
Some considered the call, but rejected it as false
The tears flowed rich and touched my dad
Some went to investigate but I answered the call
Gave myself to be loved
I am the wanted child
I was called to be loved
And I live to be loved

Do you want to be me?
You can for this journey
The choice is yours
To be the wanted child
Make me your headstone
Wear me if you choose
I am here to be worn
LOVE TO YOU ALWAYS
LOVE TO ALL ALWAYS

3 THE DREAM CHILD

She knew what she wanted
And made herself ready
The child of her dream
Her dream of a child
Her dream came true
I am her dream child
She is my dream mum

She got what she wanted
I got what I wanted
Her dream is in me
My dream is in her

Do you want to be me?
You can for this journey but the choice is yours
Wear me if you choose, make me your headstone
The choice is yours, to be me or not to be
LOVE TO YOU ALWAYS
LOVE TO ALL ALWAYS

4 THE ABORTED CHILD

I'm alive in her, whenever she thinks of me
She reads abortion, I come straight to mind
She is my mother, I chose her

She was looking for herself
And then she found me, growing in her womb
She did not choose me, she was not ready
I happened to be ready and gave it a go

She kept me a secret, pain ate her away
She did not want this position, she did not plan it
She tortured herself with all sorts of blame
The secrecy killed her, the shame buried her

She knew all the teachings, she knew the right thing
She wanted to be right but then became wrong
She was not righteous, she took all the blame
It was all her fault, that I came to be

I saw her in the midnight torturing herself
Sometimes she was covered with tears and with blood
I was alive in her, I experienced her womb
She was finding herself, not looking for a baby
She was learning to live and also to relate

A day or two earlier, a day or 2 later, it would not have happened
But it did happen and now I live in her
I also live on earth, my flesh with the soil, my blood in water

Some lives are brief, some lives are long
My life in the womb was not full term
Outside the womb, I span eternity

It was not easy for mum, it was not easy for me
We shared experience, we shared our blood
We shared our tears, we had ourselves

The struggle was fierce
I understand mum, the way no one does
I lived in mum's thoughts and also in her body, for all of

those tough times
Our struggle became the bond
The bond unseen
Mum lives in me and I live in her memory

Mum is not bad, she just was not ready
Not ready for me, not ready at that time
Mum rejects herself from time to time
I remain by mum and accept my mum when she rejects
herself

Do you want to be me?
Or do you want to be mum?
Or even the dad who does not feature at all?
You can for this journey but the choice is yours
Wear me if you choose, make me your headstone
The choice is yours, to be me or not to be
LOVE TO YOU ALWAYS
LOVE TO ALL ALWAYS

5 THE SACRED CHILD

I am the wanted one who did not take breath
I am the unwanted one who did not take breath
I am the dream one who did not take breath
I did not take breath but I am still here
Mum and I experienced me living in her womb
The time was sacred so treat it as sacred

I am the one some call stillborn
I am the one which left incomplete
The earth called me because it needed me
To complete the rest and that is complete

I am not still, I am sacred
I am not incomplete, I am infinite

Do you want to be me?
You can for this journey
Wear me if you choose, make me your headstone
The choice is yours, to be me or not to be
LOVE TO YOU ALWAYS
LOVE TO ALL ALWAYS

6   YET TO BE CONCEIVED

I am the one who does not want to take form
I am the one who is not ready to take form
I am the one considering whether to take form
I have seen the pain a form can bring
I have seen the adventure possible in a form

Do you want to be me?
You certainly can
In this journey of choice
Wear me if you choose, make me your headstone
The choice is yours, to be me or not to be
LOVE TO YOU ALWAYS
LOVE TO ALL ALWAYS

7   THE OPENING

In every journey, we construct and reconstruct as many times as
the opening demands. In a journey of books, books reconceive
themselves. We have now reached that stage of the journey, the
stage of deconstruction, reconstruction and construction. You
always have a choice to deconstruct and reconstruct or to refuse to

accept the fact. The fact that change is happening, happening now and all the time. Happening in you. Happening here. Happening there. Nothing is set unmoved, even things set in stone. Books are set to open. Books are set to move. Books are set to change. Books adapt to change. Are you such a book? A book set to move? Are you set in stone? Are you set to open? In every opening, we construct to open, we reconstruct to open, we deconstruct to open, to fit into the opening, to move and become an opening. But which is the book? Which is the opening? The opening which opens to publish.

LOVE TO YOU ALWAYS
LOVE TO ALL ALWAYS

WHAT I THOUGHT AT THIS POINT

Which is the opening? Which is the book? What kind of writing am I? In what language am I written? What am I wearing? Am I an opening? Am I the book? Can you read me? Do you understand me? I am trying to read you but do not yet understand. What are you wearing? Can you help me understand? Are you an opening? Are you a book?
  LOVE TO YOU ALWAYS
  LOVE TO ALL ALWAYS

BOOK 15
CONCEPTIONS

THE UNIVERSAL STATE OF LOVE

The earth is the space where spirits take form
Spirits of trees, land and sea
Spirits of ants, humans and birds

They come to take form to see and be seen
They come to take form to relate with other forms
To beam their LOVE in earth's full view
To express themselves fully in view
Touching where they are and where they are not

Humans once thought the earth was flat
That may be so where foot prints are flat
The earth is only flat where feet rest flat
Human feet move from space to space
And some feet move with great sense of importance
As if the whole universe is planned around them
So when some meet mountain in landscape
Towering in glory, the spirit form on earth
Or the storm of life displaying its beauty
They sigh and hiss, exasperated also
'God tests me' some proclaim at times
As though God has nothing better to do

This sense of importance is what makes some humans cruel
Thinking they're better than others whom they meet
They block intelligence and activate cruelty
Where flowers blossom, radiate and spread beauty
Some humans sit to brew, poison bombs to kill

Some humans even think universe revolves round them
And everything lined up, put in place just for them
So they conceive creator who is as they are
And as their want
Giving it all the attributes they want creator to have
As limited in scope as the mind of conception
Like-minded creator, spitting image of own mind
A creator like them with world domination in mind

Spitting image of power which they crave to have and use
A creator like its creator, they give birth to image
And give it grand name to reflect own image
And sense of importance, including cruelty
They set about to worship this image of themselves
And punish and kill those who do not think like them

This sense of importance blocks intelligence called LOVE
The intelligence inbuilt in every human form
To make humans know what other creatures know
The unseen force which other creatures see
Other creatures see what humans cannot see
Other creatures hear what humans cannot hear
Other creatures sense what humans cannot sense
The scents other beings sense humans cannot smell

The earth is the space spirits come to take form
The earth is the space beings come to be seen
The earth is the place spirits take different forms
To meet other spirits in physical forms

The earth does not revolve around humans
The earth does not belong to the human shape
The only thing that humans may call their own
Is the human shape spirits reside in and move
And the human mind thoughts reside in to express
The same really goes for other beings
Elephants, rivers, rats and things in space
Occupy a space in shape at given times

Thoughts in mind are private in nature
For each to enjoy to heart's content
The beauty of the mind for each to make

Freedom to create private garden in mind
No policing there, no censorship or rules
Each human mind is free to conceive own God
Each human mind in deed do conceive own God
Some similar in nature no conception the same
No particular rule, minds are not uniform
Thoughts made in own image, some in the image of others

Each human shape takes up space on earth
But only occupies one space at a time
Some spirits on earth exhibit themselves in human form
Their acts and expressions radiate through the human shape

One spirit all humans have and also share in common
Is also a state all beings share in common
A state which human beings call LOVE
The state of LOVE is universal in nature
Universal State of LOVE unites all in LOVE

The earth is the space where spirits take form
Spirits of trees, land and sea
Spirits of ants, humans and birds
They come to take form to see and be seen
They come to take form to relate with other forms
To beam their LOVE in earth's full view
To express themselves fully in view
Touching where they are and where they are not
LOVE TO YOU ALWAYS
LOVE TO ALL ALWAYS

WHAT I THOUGHT AT THIS POINT

I am happy to be in this state. The universal state of LOVE where beings come to take form and interact with other forms. I wonder if you can see my form. What form have I taken? What do you see? Where does the universal state of LOVE begin? Where does it end? How do I know I am in it? How do I know I have left it? Do I ever leave it once I have entered it? Does it admit of both the seen and the unseen, the form and the formless?

Come my dear friend. There is more to see. This is getting more exciting. Let's journey more into the unknown.

BOOK 16

THE BOOK OF TOUCH LOVE

Touch LOVE

A concept, a solution, a philosophy, a way of life rooted in LOVE
To touch LOVE is to allow the LOVE within to connect with the
LOVE in all things
By so connecting, LOVE flows freely to produce the LOVE-
induced advancement of the human intellect and the LOVE-
induced expansion of the human mind and the LOVE-induced
evolution of humanity

THE BOOK OF TOUCH LOVE is about the State of LOVE.
The state of all things and all beings.

The aim of the book is to inspire readers to look through the
lens of all things, not just own things, through the spectacles of all
beings, not just human beings. It is a book which does not look
down on things but sees things as important as non-things, sees
humans as important as non-humans, sees seen as important as
unseen and sees it as important as she and he.

LOVE is a thing and a non-thing, that thing and non-thing
present in she, in he, in all, so is bigger than a he, and larger than a
she and more expanse and limitless than all.

The book of Touch LOVE is a book of philosophy which approaches all things through the centre of LOVE and recognises LOVE as the centre of all things and of all non-things. The centre from which all emanate as rays of LOVE radiating in nothingness. The core of all things from which all things evolve and around which all revolve.

Touch LOVE is not a philosophy focusing on individuals or on human models. Its focus is on the intangible model which models all things and all beings into a state of LOVE. The intangible model is the state of LOVE.

The philosophy proceeds from the idea that the State of LOVE is the Supreme State in which every being thrives, every intelligence grows, every beauty expands, every uniqueness compliments and is harmonised, and every channel of beauty opens wide to connect, and the connection expands intelligence and moves and excites spirits. It is a philosophy of the movement of LOVE. A philosophy which does not look down on things and does not look down on non-things. Everything starts from a non-thing and every something was once a nothing. It is an idea which looks up in awe to all things and to non-things to learn about things and to know own self.

LOVE TO YOU ALWAYS
LOVE TO ALL ALWAYS

BOOK 17

AN ESTABLISHMENT OF LOVE

The song we heard as we entered this space

LOVE is food and must not be the preserve of a few
LOVE is power which all can exercise
LOVE is nourishment which all beings need
LOVE is energy which powers creation of beauty
LOVE is invisible which heals the visible
LOVE is sustenance which each can cultivate
LOVE nourishes the mind, the spirit and the body
LOVE nurtures intellect and expands understanding
An establishment of LOVE expresses words produced by LOVE
An establishment of LOVE takes actions powered by LOVE
So establish LOVE where there is no LOVE
Establish rule of LOVE and make it visible
Law has been visible in all places it rules
It is only LOVE which makes good law
But LOVE remains invisible where it ought to be visible
In governments, in parliaments, in offices, at work
In law books, in politics, in management, in court
But LOVE is the invisible which makes many law

unnecessary
LOVE is the food which the mind of government needs
So in every action, please ask yourself these
Does this represent the LOVE in me and in all things?
Does this present LOVE to me and to all things?
Does this express LOVE for all beings?
Does this destroy me or any other being?
Does this nourish me and all touched by it?
LOVE is food which nourishes all
LOVE must not be the preserve of a few
LOVE is power which all can exercise
LOVE is health care and ought be central to all care
LOVE TO YOU ALWAYS
LOVE TO ALL ALWAYS

An establishment of LOVE institutes LOVE as the leader of all thoughts, expressions and actions. An institute of LOVE is a school of Touch LOVE. The school of Touch LOVE creates awareness of the two states of the human mind namely the state of LOVE and the state of lack of LOVE.

There are varying degrees of the state of lack of LOVE. The degrees depend on the amount of residual LOVE in a being. Where a being operates on very restricted LOVE to vital organs, the lack of LOVE in those organs causes extensive damage and destruction to the being and to all around. Where the supply of LOVE is intermittently disrupted by blockages and experiences, the interruptions cause intermittent destructive thoughts which can lead to destructive acts. By recognising this state of affairs, individuals are equipped with the knowledge with which to decide whether or not to solve own problems. Understanding the incidence and occurrence of lack of LOVE energy creates a new terminology of 'state of LOVE' and 'state of lack of LOVE' which in itself focuses minds on the actual cause of destructive acts and expressions.

This book is a school of Touch LOVE which aims to help individuals unblock blocked channels of LOVE by refocusing minds and intellects on LOVE and shining away anti-LOVE notions which have been stifling LOVE growth of human societies and restricting LOVE expansion in minds.

Lack of LOVE causes intermittent destructive thoughts and acts. When there is a better understanding of LOVE and its energy, individuals can relate better to themselves. To touch LOVE is a self-help system which all can operate. Armed with the right knowledge and awareness, each individual can identify their own state of LOVE and their own state of depleting LOVE, relate better with own self and become more aware of what to do when own supply of LOVE is running low.

Each individual can and is encouraged to diagnose own self so as to take immediate steps to resolve any issue which has the potential of possibly blocking a pore of LOVE or destroying a channel of LOVE. By looking inwards to identify emerging potential LOVE blockages, each individual may choose to act quickly to ensure that the potential blockage is not allowed to fester, take root and block the radiance of LOVE. Where possible the individual will take steps towards removing any root which has already clogged up the pore of LOVE, then follow this up by refilling self with LOVE. A LOVE-filled being overflows in LOVE, and in that being, LOVE has a prime and supreme place.

There are diverse LOVE-filling stations to which an individual may connect to refuel in LOVE. Refilling self with LOVE reinstates thinking through LOVE, acting through LOVE, being in LOVE. It is LOVE-overflow which creates an aura of LOVE around an individual, generates the state of oneness with all LOVEbeings and establishes a state of euphoria in an individual's world.

This book helps individuals to find the LOVE-filling stations nearest to them and to understand how to connect to refill self with LOVE. It is the first publicly available compilation of Touch LOVE thoughts and ideas. It is a Touch LOVE clinic and LOVE-filling station in itself and constitutes a proposal to the world to adopt LOVE as the supreme leader. If LOVE is instituted as the leader in all spheres of human activity, the world would be a world of LOVE and human behaviour will ascend to the state of LOVE always.

This book poses these questions. Are you really interested in living in a world of LOVE? A world ruled by LOVE. Are you really interested in doing what it takes to create a world ruled by LOVE? Studying yourself deeply to recognise when you are in a state of overflowing LOVE and when your LOVE supply is in a depleting state. Will you adopt LOVE as your personal leader in all things? Practising LOVE in all strands of living including in all leadership and governance, in all courts and schools, in all organisations and establishments, making LOVE the SUPREME teacher, healer and leader.

This book proposes that the course of Touch LOVE be taught in all educational and health institutions at every level from ante-natal clinics to tertiary institutions and beyond. The course will assist individuals who are minded to create a world of LOVE to know how to go about it. This book encourages Touch LOVE discussions to take place formally and informally, at places of work and places of leisure, at home and outside the home.

LOVE is the thing that makes lasting positive change. It is the thing which creates world peace. It is in the state of LOVE that individual intellectual brilliance soars to those unprecedented heights which beautify all around.

This book invites the world to look into LOVE with a view to establishing departments of Touch LOVE. It encourages governments to establish a Ministry of Touch LOVE and asks individuals to consider adopting the practice of LOVE in all they do. LOVE prevents all kinds of destructions and heals wounded minds. LOVE is a fundamental food and nutrition, an intangible energy which provides fulfilment, contentment, satisfaction and peace of mind.

The fuel LOVE supplies sustains minds, inspires spirits, nourishes intellects and beautifies the body.

Every being has some LOVE though LOVE levels differ. This fundamental fact is what this book is giving prominence. When LOVE is seen as food, attitudes to LOVE may change and this change may change the way each individual lives.

THE SUPREME STATE OF LOVE

To touch LOVE is to ascend into the Supreme State of LOVE. The process of ascension begins when a being looks inwards to find the LOVE within. When a being finds the LOVE within, the being has connected with the LOVE within. To connect with the LOVE within is to connect with the LOVE in all things.

Upon connecting with LOVE, the LOVE within begins to glow and radiate until it reaches full power. No being can contain the full radiation of the LOVE within. So the radiation beams through every pore, wall, boundary and every outlet of the being. That beaming out is called reaching out. When LOVE reaches out, it touches everything on its radiating path. It can transform touched faces into smiles. It can transform troubled minds into peace of mind.

Flowers touch LOVE when their buds open up wide to fully connect with elements and when perfumes are released from deep within plants. The sun touches LOVE when the particles of its internal combustion travels millions of light years to permeate the earth and touch earth beings. It is the beam of LOVE which calms the spirit when one beholds a tranquil stream. It is the beam of LOVE which produces a lift when one gazes at the awe-inspiring mountain. In humans, the touch of LOVE opens to the full the valve of LOVE within, letting it flow through every pore, point and outlet, to reach out to connect into the LOVE in all things.

In the state of LOVE, supreme intellectual state is reached, harmony of uniqueness is perceived, beauty and fluidity inspire progress, productivity grows to last, ecstatic excitement nourishes to expand, the state of euphoria is cultivated and produces an aura of LOVE, peace of mind and world peace.

Only LOVE produces LOVE and only LOVE generates LOVE energy. When human intellect is exercised by only LOVE, it expands into unimaginable realms of LOVE, creating beauty as it unfolds and moving humans away from sporadic acts of destruction. LOVE repairs what has been destroyed. This is why it is so important for countries to invest in LOVE and establish LOVE institutions.

LOVE TO YOU ALWAYS
LOVE TO ALL ALWAYS

WHAT I THOUGHT AT THIS POINT

What a LOVE song!
Did you sing along to it?
Look over there!
What is that emerging?
Come let's go and find out.

BOOK 18

THE BOOK OF ABILITY

ABILITY
Is that your name?
Are you a book?
A book called Ability?
What ability do you have?
The ability of LOVEbearing?
The ability of you and mc?
How much LOVE do you bear?
How much LOVE bears you?
How able are you?
How able in LOVE?
How connected are you?
How connected to LOVE?
As you connect through
I hope you connect with me
Connecting to the LOVE I bear
The ability in me
The ability I bear
The ability in you
The ability you bear
The ability to bear LOVE
The ability to LOVE all

The ability which bears us
And lifts us high
Into the state of LOVE
LOVE TO YOU ALWAYS
LOVE TO ALL ALWAYS

LACK OF LOVE

You have heard of lack of money. You have heard of lack of food. But have you heard of lack of LOVE? The condition known as lack of LOVE. The disability called lack of LOVE. That is what this book is about. It is here to tell you about lack of LOVE.

Many are struggling in life because of 'lack of LOVE'. Lack of LOVE is different from lack of money. It is different from mental illness. And also different from lacking a job. Lack of LOVE is a serious condition. It can destroy the sufferer and others near the sufferer.

A mentally ill person may be full of LOVE. A mentally well person may be lacking in LOVE. A jobless person may be full of LOVE. An employed person may be lacking in LOVE. A person with no money may be full of LOVE. A person with money, may be lacking in LOVE. A new term is born in this book. Its name is 'Lack of LOVE'. The terminology will now be *"I am in the state of lack of LOVE", "Trying to get to the state of full of LOVE", "I do not want to change state. What is wrong with the state of lack of LOVE"*.

This book of ability focuses on ability. The ability to LOVE and to receive LOVE. Many are able to LOVE because they are in 'full LOVE'. Some are in 'new LOVE' and others in 'half-LOVE'. Some are in 'quarter-LOVE' whilst others are LOVE crescents. Some are 'LOVE active' whilst some are 'LOVE disabled'. Each will LOVE according to own level and degree of LOVE.

This book highlights the disability known as 'lack of LOVE'. Sometimes certain circumstances disable LOVE connection in certain aspects of an individual's life. Depending on its degree, when LOVE is not supplied to aspects of an individual's life, the lack of LOVE in those aspects can be a very disabling condition. It is more so when swept under the carpet, is misdiagnosed and not seen for what it is.

The term 'lack of LOVE' is relatively unknown and many who suffer this disability do not know it. Some do not have the ability to recognise or to accept that they suffer it, at the time they are suffering it. Many who have the ability to recognise the disabling condition of lack of LOVE, do not want to let go of the disability. Some have a need to hold on to the disability even when they have the ability to let go of it. This makes lack of LOVE a very complex condition to address. So the place of this book is in the prevention space. Preventing incidents of disabling lack of LOVE.

The prevention space is any space where beings meet to encourage each other to LOVE. LOVE is the preventative medicine. Taking a course of preventative medicine is hoped to help reduce future incidents of that disability known as lack of LOVE.

Many humans live a life of 'full LOVE' and do not destroy themselves or others, but from time to time some may suffer an attack of lack of LOVE. Like many attacks, the attacked may have home-brewed medicine which soothes and heals, so does not need a hospital or assistance from another. Sometimes a person who suffers an attack of lack of LOVE may need to speak to somebody. Speaking to somebody, in itself, becomes a cure. In speaking to somebody, the speaker hears own voice and works out how to resolve the matter.

Many attacks of lack of LOVE can be treated if the sufferer is willing to have it treated. The basic state of being is the state of equilibrium from where beings take off to the state of LOVE or degenerate into the state of lack of LOVE. When an attack of lack of LOVE is treated, the being returns to the state of equilibrium from where the being can take off to the state of LOVE, moved by LOVE.

The state of LOVE is the supreme state of being for any being. It is the state of being to which most beings aspire to reach and remain in. However, this is not always reached because from time to time circumstances create a state of intermittent destructive situations which strike individuals and disrupt thoughts, producing diverse emotional responses. Some of the responses erupt as actions of the individuals. This state of affairs can be a draw back to the individual's movement to the state of LOVE but may also be its catalyst. It is a draw back when the negative thoughts and emotions are not immediately addressed and go on to produce more destructive thoughts which take root, and control the individual's mind and actions, damaging peace of mind and consequently damaging peace in the individual's world, and in some cases, spilling out of the individual's world into the collective world, damaging and destroying all on its path. Experiencing intermittent disruptions may be a catalyst moving an individual to the state of LOVE when an individual acts against the instincts to react destructively, and in its stead, reacts LOVINGLY, turning what would have been destructive thoughts into healing creative thoughts which create beauty out of the destructive situations, radiating LOVE which beautifies all on its path.

TOUCH LOVE CENTRES

To reduce lack of LOVE disability, this book proposes that communities establish Touch LOVE centres throughout all community centres and hospitals, libraries and schools, streets and public transport stations. It does not take much to establish

TOUCH LOVE CENTRES in these existing spaces. It only takes conviction in the benefits such centres will bring, passion for that benefit, determination to secure that benefit and cooperation with others in bringing about that benefit. The centres serve to make individuals more aware of their ability to reduce incidents of lack of LOVE and will encourage the use of the new terminology as there will be an exhibition in the centres of the new terms of 'lack of LOVE', 'full LOVE', 'LOVEbearer' and other Touch LOVE terms.

SELF-HELP

Touch LOVE development is about individuals allowing the LOVE in them and around them to develop their intellect by allowing LOVE to occupy, possess, energise and expand their minds. It is about allowing LOVE to exercise the intellect and allowing own intellect to keep exploring ways of opening up to the full, the valve of LOVE within.

Touch LOVE is the practice of touching, stirring and invoking the LOVE within until it radiates beyond the boundaries of the body and the form to connect with the LOVE in other forms and bodies. When humans touch LOVE, LOVE expands the human mind into realms of LOVE and transforms the human mind into a LOVE-magnetic space of nothingness, picking up LOVE signals and bearing only that which is LOVE. In that state, only LOVE induces and inspires thoughts and actions. In that state, a being gravitates towards LOVE always.

LOVEBEARER

Central to the concept of Touch LOVE is the idea that every being, animate and inanimate, is a 'LOVEbearer' with equal direct access and connectivity to LOVE just as those who breathe have equal direct access and connectivity to the air they breathe. A LOVEbearer as an entity bears LOVE, has invisible points into which the invisible LOVE connects, and reflects LOVE as mirrors reflect light and images.

Bearing LOVE means that LOVE particles are in that being and LOVE energy is stored in that being. The stored LOVE energy can be touched and when touched it can glow and start to expand. From a glow of LOVE it can expand to a beam of LOVE. From a beam of LOVE, it can expand to star LOVE, shining through and radiating beyond the being, emitting the warmth of LOVE and transmitting LOVE in the frequency of LOVE. Bearing LOVE also means that the being bears LOVE as trees bear fruits and as beings give birth to babies. It means that the being multiplies endlessly in LOVE.

The LOVE in each LOVEbearer can increase and overflow to create an aura of LOVE around the LOVEbearer, shielding the LOVEbearer from that which is not LOVE, shining away what is not LOVE and beautifying all on the LOVEbearer's path.

Being a LOVEbearer does not mean that the LOVEbearer is always filled to the brim with LOVE. Just as the LOVE in an entity can increase, filling up the entity to overflowing proportion, so can the level of LOVE in an entity drop and continuously decrease. Circumstances may block the artery of LOVE causing LOVE depletion in parts of the body and causing the entity to wither and die from the disease of lack of LOVE.

DESERT LACK OF LOVE

The drying out of LOVE creates a destructive state called 'Desert lack of LOVE' which is different from 'intermittent lack of LOVE'. Intermittent lack of LOVE creates sporadic acts of destruction.

Desert lack of LOVE destroys everything on its path including the faculties which perceive LOVE. At this level and degree of lack of LOVE, a being lacks an ability to resurrect itself as the lack of LOVE has destroyed all the faculties within the being which internally self-trigger a glow of LOVE. In this state of being, the being's own ability to touch LOVE from within is disabled from within. Only a continuous rain of LOVE from outside the being can penetrate the being with a flood of LOVE. However there comes a stage when the lack of LOVE seals the being tight and impenetrable so that no amount of LOVE rain can penetrate into the being.

Intermittent lack of LOVE is different from desert lack of LOVE because at the intermittent stage the being retains an ability to heal itself from within. Many LOVEbearers whose LOVE level is low have the ability to connect to LOVE and refill their LOVE to overflowing proportion.

LOVE SPEAK

Touch LOVE solution is a course of preventative medicine. It reminds people that LOVE has its own language and invites people to adopt the language of LOVE and speak LOVE.

Communication is important and is a fundamental part of Touch LOVE therapy. Many humans choose violence as their way of communicating. Violence is a destructive way of communicating. Some humans choose debating as a way of communicating. Debates are good but have been known to create an atmosphere of hostility, batter and entrenched positions, with a focus on winning the argument not building a bridge of LOVE. Taking sides, exposing weaknesses and inflicting the greatest damage to an opposing side is not a method of communication which opens up minds. It does not always build bridges of understanding between arguing sides even though banter is sometimes employed to soften some blows.

The book of Ability is a book with the aim of building bridges of LOVE in communities, across differences, between individuals, nations, cultures, customs and practices. The only language necessary to achieve the cross is the language of LOVE. It is hoped that many may find what is written in this book useful and engage well with the Touch LOVE solution and concept.

The **LOVE SPEAK** is already happening. Expanding involvement in the 'Touch LOVE' conversation presently happening around the world is one purpose of this book. It is hoped that governments, educational institutions, health institutions, commercial establishments, legal justice systems and individuals from all backgrounds will engage with the conversation and express themselves as moved.

Conversations create and promote understanding if people are determined to engage in the discussion of difficult issues in a spirit of LOVE and understanding. Engaging with difficult issues is very necessary and so is approaching them in a relaxed non-confrontational way. Such approach yields an exchange of ideas if participants see themselves as people on one side, the side of LOVE, united by one goal, the goal of building bridges of LOVE. If participants see hostility as the enemy, they will be united against hostility and be in harmony on the side of LOVE, enjoying and cherishing the exhibition of each participant's unique thought and mannerism. Engaging with difficult issues in this way has the potential of preventing situations of hostility and conflict from ever developing, if conversations are held frequently, when no conflict is in sight.

Time invested in holding regular conversations is time well spent in preventing future destructions. Inability to maintain regular exchange of ideas breeds many destructive situations because lack of conversation breeds misunderstandings which go on to create assumptions and hostility. Lack of LOVE creates destructive thoughts which if not aired, heard and addressed, would fester unaddressed and may end up destroying sufferer and those around. Conversation is very important because it draws out destructive thoughts, and LOVE can shine upon the thoughts and transform them into things of beauty. When destructive thoughts are heard, steps can be taken to address the root of the lack of LOVE before it grows into a tree of destruction.

A tree of destruction is a tree of lack of LOVE bearing lack of LOVE branches. Lack of LOVE and its branches block connections, close minds, cause stinginess, perpetuate oppression and all kinds of slavery, violence, destructive discrimination, maltreatment, abuse, hardness of heart and destroy the sufferer as well as others.

Exchange of ideas is an openness which has the potential to open minds to LOVE. So honesty and genuine interest in building a bridge of LOVE is the key to a successful Touch LOVE conversation. A mistake of facts can be an honest mistake which was not intended to mislead but which was believed to be correct at the time the mistake was made. However, sharing of ideas and information is defeated if it is only done as a lip service or box ticking exercise with no genuine intention to engage or any interest in building a bridge of LOVE. It is counter-productive and deceitful to participate in a Touch LOVE conversation laden with an intention to misrepresent facts and then go ahead to actually misrepresent facts intending to mislead and manipulate.

The ability to LOVE is the ability which every being has because LOVE energy is stored in every being and when touched, it stars LOVE, radiating LOVE worldwide, finding expression in the language of LOVE, healing, building and beautifying the being and all on its path.

All beings living on land have the ability to LOVE. The sea and the beings living in water have the ability to LOVE. Mountains have the ability to LOVE. The atmosphere itself has the ability to LOVE. If humans invest in their ability to LOVE, there will be less incidents of lack of LOVE disabilities in the humans of now and of the future.

LOVE TO YOU ALWAYS
LOVE TO ALL ALWAYS

WHAT I THOUGHT AT THIS POINT

I have been thinking of what you said at BOOK 16
If you recall, I was silent, listening intently to what you were saying
Is my understanding correct?
Did you really mean that BOOK 16 is a book about talking to yourself?
A book about me talking to myself?
Why talk to myself when I can talk to you?
Why look into myself when I can look into others?
These thoughts have been troubling me since I left BOOK 16
Then BOOK one eight comes along telling me to talk to others
To have a conversation
To realise that I have ability which can become disabled
But do I have the ability to.....

Look! Look! Look!
Look over there! To where I am pointing
It looks like that unfolding something we could not make out from a distance
The emerging scene we saw unfolding from far away!
We seem to now be only few breaths away from it
Let's not run out of breath my dear friend
But let's run to find out

Let's see what that unknown holds

Goodbye BOOK 18
You have been most entertaining
Thanks for all that you have displayed
We are thinking about them
And will continue to talk about them
LOVE TO YOU ALWAYS
LOVE TO ALL ALWAYS

BOOK 19

THE NAMELESS

A SONG ACCOMPANIED BY MUSICAL INSTRUMENTS

Anyo   Anyo
Anyo   Anyo
Anyo Anyo Anyo Anyo Anyo Anyo
Anyo Anyo Anyo Anyo Anyo Anyo

THE STORY AS TOLD

The day was sunny, airy and warm. Three nameless seeds were attached to a tree. They have always been part of this tree. They were fed and nurtured like every part of the tree. Sunshine reached them and touched them. When it rained, they were touched too. From their places of attachment, they would survey their surroundings, watching the goings on and watching all around them. Below them was the fertile soil, always heaving a song or two. On this particular day, the three nameless seeds heard the fertile song heaving this song:

Make me your home
Put root in me
Sprout in me and grow

Stretch stem and branch
To reach the sky
Make me your home
My dream will be realised

Above them were the clouds dancing to the heaving soil. Some birds were in formations, displaying spectacular acrobatic dances. Some other birds were on branches, land and hills, thrusting their heads forward and back and chanting....

Impossible
Mhu
Becomes possible
Mhu
Impossible
Mhu
Becomes possible
Mhu
Impossible, becomes possible
In LOVE all is possible
Mhu mhu mhuhuhu mhu...

The show was spectacular and captivating. The enchanting beauty created a magnetic aura, pulling all around to participate in the show. So the mountain joined in. Its awesomeness towered and beamed. The sea was in an extraordinary spirit. Its waves rose to unprecedented heights. The tranquil stream could not resist the bewitching scene, so it joined in too but it did not change its nature. It remained tranquil. Its beauty became more enhanced by its exhibition of the reflection of the beauty of the waving trees flanking its banks. Some of the trees were big and some small, some with huge visible roots and others with branches which have made themselves into living bridges curving over the stream. The stream nodded and undulated, adding its sound to the music. It was indeed happy. It was beaming with joy and all around could see that. It appeared in all its glory, reflecting the beauty of the beings which are in it. The sun which had been smiling the whole time, was now dancing on the surface of the stream, creating beautiful patterns of shimmer which bounce off in different directions in dazzling brilliance. Where the stream was more still, it became a mirror to all who went to look into its stillness.

The long river could not resist the pull and came out like a travelling lightning sparkling in the distance. It elegantly displayed the beauty of its meandering course, curving its way around obstacles which stood to be noticed. The desert was not left out as it stirred to life to display the beauty of its dust in different arrays of lights and settled to colour and paint everything that came to it to rest.

The pull of this beautiful atmospheric scene was getting to those three nameless seeds attached to a tree. The captivating scene captured their attention and the pull became increasingly irresistible. But detachment is a very painful process even when it happens when it should happen. Even at a ripe stage, detaching from the known to an unknown is not an easy detachment. Moving away from a habit of watching to a dance step of a new does not come that easy. The seeds were ripe and were detaching. They were detaching when they should be detaching. The enchanting irresistible magnetic aura distracted them from themselves and pulled them on until they detached. The three of them. They found themselves floating away from their bearer.

The first seed was fully engaged with that dance and music which distracted it from itself. It was captured by the unfolding wonder and beauty. Its dream mode was activated and dreams welled up uncontrollably. It felt itself melt into nothingness, then felt itself expand endlessly to a state where all dreams became reality and all things became possible. Images of beauty paraded by in what seemed like an endless unfolding of beauty. The captivating beauty stirred up words which took form, then the form took a life of its own and erupted to the open to be noticed.

"EBUKA!!!!!!!!!!"

Was the eruption which came emanating from the first nameless seed. It was an explosion of passion. But this sound which emanated from it, shook it. A wonder in itself, which it did not think possible. The nameless seed never knew it could make sound.

"EBUKA!!!!" Again erupted uncontrollably from within the first nameless seed and echoed beyond. Its breath has formed the emotion welling up within it into an eruption of words flowing out of it into the open.

"EBUKA!!!"

More words uncontrollably erupted and flowed in the form of a chant…

"Call me EBUKA
You invited me to make this soil my home
I will make this soil my home
Your dream is mine too
I will try my best in everything
My roots will reach deep inside of you and go farther in
search of nourishment
Nourishment to make me BIG
I will sprout huge branches that spread over the land
My flowers will release scents which the wind will carry
far and near
A different scent for a different season

I will be home to birds
And all kinds of beings will call me home
In me would be found variety of food to feed variety of
beings
Fruits, leaves, roots, vegetables
Sustenance for all, big or small
I will be many trees in one
I have today taken a name
I am no longer a nameless seed
I am Ebuka, the many in one
So call me EBUKA, EbuMany
EBUKA! Many in one tree!!!!

The second seed was in the same dream state as Ebuka and could not hold back the erupting words flowing into the open…

"From now on, I will be known as Mma
I will try my best in everything
I will be home to butterflies, to all little beings
Yellowish leaves will be part of me
Red leaves will be part of me
And so would green and brown
I would be a tree of many colours
Bees will make their home in me
Flowers will bloom diverse beauty
Not one kind but many kinds
Not one fold but many folds
Rippling in colours and in sizes
The sight of me will produce exclamations
Beholders of me will remain in awe
And smile will bloom and warmth will glow
'What a beauty-FULL tree' many will stop and say
Call me Mma, the one full of beauty

Call me Mma, the diverse beauty
Call me Mma, many varieties-in-one
Call me Mma, the one full in beauty

A chant is heard from all around in harmony.

EbuMany in one tree
Mma, the beautiful diversity

The rain sprinkled its water on all, refreshing and energising all as it danced along. The mountains echoed, the leaves rustled, streams chorused, the thunder clapped, the birds chirped, all in harmony, none dominating the chant.

As Ebuka and Mma were possessed by the spirit of their dance, twirling and gyrating uncontrollably, they heard a harsh and coarse thunder piercing through the atmospheric scene, interrupting the beautiful harmony and disrupting the enriching chant. This thunder which had come to add its voice to the show was a different thunder from the beautiful one which clapped an accompaniment to the rain and the lightning. It was not the same clapping one chanting with the rest. This thunder was different. It was not clapping. It was erupting and spilling these:

"Fools! You TWO are fools!!!"
"What is wrong with both of you?
Have you lost your minds?
Or is it that you are seeds with no minds
Be REAL, dreams are not real!
In all your time hanging on the bearer and watching goings on, did you not hear passers-by say that dreams are for fools?
And right they were!
Dreams are for fools!

Escape routes from reality NOT to reality!
Oh, how I hate all these dancing and music making
Merry making for fools with no future!
You have just detached from the bearer
Your future if you have one remains unknown
Do you not understand your present situation is one of near death?
Why am I caught up in this foolish and meaningless exhibition of passion!
A complete waste of time and energy!
Do you not know this music?
Here at this time, dead at the next!
That is the music of here

'Dreaming seeds' how ridiculous
No matter how much you dream
No matter how much work you put in
You could never be what you dream
You are seeds!!!
Seeds! Seeds! Seeds!
Do you not get it?
Homeless and floating
Those chanting birds will soon swoop
And you end up between their beaks
Those exhibiting waters would soon turn
And you would end up being swept away
You think those other unknown beings are your friends
because they are cheering you on?
They are the ones to crush you!!!
Do you not get it?
You are seeds without home
Seeds detached from home!
Seeds without family

Wandering with no protection
Do you not know this music?
Here at this time, dead at the next!
That is the music of here.

What use is trying your best when your best would come
to nothing
It is madness to carry on as you have being doing
Taking grand names for yourselves
EBUKA, MANY IN ONE!
MMA, FULL IN BEAUTY!
How foolish!
Labouring under the weight of TITLES bigger than you
are
I shall take no name
I remain how I am
No name!
I remain nameless!
Otumdi
Just as I am
I remain the same
I bear no name
Call me no name!"

It was the third seed thundering and storming. At that very moment when Ebuka and Mma realised that it was the third seed storming, a real angry thunder roared, followed by a great storm. Everything changed. Trees were harassed and felled. The sea was turbulent, clashed and roared. The wind swept up large objects and crashed them into others, wreaking and leaving destruction as it moved. Its force lifted all the 3 seeds and twirled them violently. This change of beat went on and on as though it will never change. But it did change. A change can change.

The storm stopped. The lightning passed. Thunder went quiet. What Otumdi said to Ebuka and Mma proved itself to be true. *Here at this time, dead at the next. The music of here.* The inspiring and magical setting which transformed Ebuka and Mma into the singing and dancing seeds was dead. Nowhere in sight. *Here at this time, dead at the next. The music of here.*

Ebuka found itself all alone in an unknown hard dark quiet place. Ebuka does not like being alone especially in a dark hard place. But there is something about this place which struck Ebuka and stirred something of beauty inside Ebuka. The something of beauty lifted Ebuka. The lift was high and the connection strong. Ebuka did not know what it was that struck it but whatever it was, it made Ebuka to feel good about itself and to beam in joy. Ebuka was alive again. Alive with dreams. Ebuka's joy spread beyond Ebuka and expanded into other worlds. The world of the past and the world of the future. Ebuka remembered the time it was still an attachment and remembered what it saw whilst attached to its bearer. Ebuka remembered the beauty of family. This beautiful thought brought with it pleasant gentle scents which soothed Ebuka and transported it into a dream state.

Ebuka was moved into a state of beauty, an experience of glow and euphoria. Though the bearer of Ebuka at that moment was hard not soft as the fertile soil which asked Ebuka to make it home, Ebuka felt at home. The whole atmosphere felt like home. It was an extraordinary experience. Ebuka was captivated by the beauty of silence having just experienced the clashing of the storm. The experience of the storm highlighted the beauty of this silence.

Whilst Ebuka was soaking in the beauty of tranquillity, it heard itself whisper: *"I LOVE this place. I LOVE this space. I wonder where I am. I wonder what it is. I wonder if it has a name. I wonder if I can move around in it. I will like to find out".* Then Ebuka remembered that it is only a seed, battered and moved by the storm and remains in the dark, not knowing where it is. Ebuka became elated at this point. It became very happy about the fact that it was only a seed but it survived the storm. At that very moment, all things became possible. Its dream of being Many-in-one returned. Ebuka became even more determined to grow up. It became curious about where it was and was determined to find out more about that place where it came alive again. Ebuka heard itself saying *"I will find out where I am. I will grow up. When I grow up, I will love to be part of the family of this hard dark quiet"*. This thought excited Ebuka to no end. Ebuka's passion soared and enlarged Ebuka. Ebuka expanded into more dream states and more dreams filtered in to be borne. Ebuka felt itself melt. It melted into nothingness and expanded in realms of nothingness until it heard the eruption coming from deep inside of it:

"I must first sprout and root in fertile soil
To grow up to be big enough to see what I cannot see at
this level
Yes, when I grow up I will return here
But I must first go on my adventure
To know where I am
So as to return to where I am
With all that I can be"

Ebuka was so happy to meet up with its dream. Its dream has not been washed away by the flood. It has not been crushed by the storm. It was not blown away by the whirlwind. Its dream returned to it and became its companion. Ebuka had lost Mma and Otumdi in the storm. Ebuka was sad about its losses but became thrilled about its findings. Ebuka's new dream became its new finding, its new source of joy. Ebuka's thoughts did not leave its dream. Ebuka was fully energised by its thoughts. Its dream was like food, supplying excitement, an extraordinary lifting energy. Ebuka was not in fertile soil so had not had the other kind of food but was still full of energy. It was filled to the brim and erupting with high energy supplied by its dream. All Ebuka's senses were activated and engaged by its dream though Ebuka had no idea of how to go about achieving its dream.

In its attempt to sense where it was, Ebuka engaged fully with the unique soothing scent of where it was. This reminded Ebuka of its ambition to make different scents for different times but did not give Ebuka any idea of where it was. What it gave Ebuka was a stir. The scent stirred something of beauty deep inside Ebuka and Ebuka glowed with joy and felt something on its skin.

It was the gentle breeze touching and caressing Ebuka's skin. Ebuka realised that breeze spreads scents and that the gentle breeze may have brought that unique soothing scent. In all that chaos of the storm, Ebuka had forgotten about the air. The air had always been Ebuka's best friend and companion. It was always with Ebuka wherever Ebuka was. Ebuka was very happy to meet up with its 2 best friends; its dream and the air. Ebuka then called upon the gentle breeze to help blow it to a fertile soil.

'Gentle breeze Gentle breeze
Steer me to a fertile soil
Gentle breeze Gentle breeze
Stir me to a place to grow'

As Ebuka sang, Ebuka heard a shout:
"Can I not get some peace!
You silly seed!
How stupid can you be?
Carrying on with your silly dream in this hard forsaken place?
How can any seed in its right scent, possibly dream in this hard place?

A hopeless hard place where nothing happens. A hopeless hard place where nothing grows."

"Otumdi is alive!" thought Ebuka.

Ebuka then heard another voice. A calm and soothing one. *"Ebuka I'm here. I'll sing with you"*. It was Mma! Ebuka was overjoyed.

Ebuka's song was the connection which connected Ebuka, Mma and Otumdi. It was the string which connected the silence and the something which stirred the voices. It was the bridge which brought the three seeds together again.

Ebuka and Mma were dancing and singing out with joy but Otumdi was thundering and ranting: *"Fools! You are both fools!!! Can't you see that we would come to nothing in this hard place"*

As Mma and Ebuka continued to sing, and Otumdi continued to rant, all three seeds felt a lift. The gentle breeze lifted them up. Ebuka and Mma experienced the lift of the most enjoyable beautiful ride they had ever experienced. Otumdi was not left out. It was equally treated to the wonderful ride even though it was protesting and grumbling. The ride of the breeze treats all on its path. Air does not discriminate and works in those who take it in. It does its sustenance work even if someone is polluting the air. So the three seeds were well treated by the breeze which gently deposited them on soil. Each landed in a different place and none knew whether the other made it to fertile soil or survived beings hunting seeds for energy.

Ebuka found itself on fertile soil. It happily sprouted whilst it sang. This enriched the neighbourhood and filled the neighbouring beings with wonder. A singing seed? Ebuka pushed out its roots and stretched far and beyond in search of food. It went over stones and under rocks. It enjoyed working hard and had great fun trying its very best. Every day was different and became an exciting adventure! Ebuka met many beings on its adventure and had many enriching conversations.

Otumdi was right when it said that beings would come to eat seeds. Beings did come to eat Ebuka but the ones which came to eat Ebuka changed their minds. They were transformed. They had not seen anything like Ebuka before and liked coming to watch Ebuka at work. Ebuka always sang and danced as it worked. It always beamed smiles as it blossomed. This cheered up all around it. Ebuka did not need protection. Its own joy protected it and made it many friends. Ebuka's friends included those beings which would ordinarily have eaten it. The amazing thing is that Ebuka's hard work captivated the beings so much that they would sit by Ebuka for a very long time and deposit their waste on the soil. Their waste was a special delicacy which nourished the soil and helped build Ebuka even stronger.

As for Otumdi it was not eaten by the beings as it predicted. The beings did not like the look of it. It was bitter and always angry. So the beings did not visit it and would go past it to visit Ebuka. You are what you eat the beings will say. They did not want to become Otumdi. They did not want to be bitter and angry. Eating Otumdi, they thought, will make them bitter and angry and breed in them bitterness and anger.

Otumdi just lay there on the soil, grumpy and unhappy. It did not bother pushing its root at all but its roots came out anyway and its stem stretched to the sun. One day, its root came upon a huge rock which was in the way of food and water but Otumdi refused to go over it or under it. Otumdi was not interested in helping itself or anybody to grow. It carried a lot of anger around. If it was not complaining about one thing, it was complaining about another. It always found the fault in things and never created or suggested solutions. It never looked happy. It wanted others to do everything and was not interested in any adventure which required it to try its best. In fact Otumdi did not like any adventure or work. Its only adventure was into anger and complaint. It would not thank you if you are kind to it and always thundered in irritation.

One day, a wanderer smelled a scent so beautiful that the wanderer was moved to begin an adventure to find the source of the scent. Wanderers do things like that. The wanderer took its family and followed the scent. The scent led them to an amazing tree. The wanderer called the tree *Many in one* because it was so big and looked like many things in one. It had different coloured leaves. It had different coloured flowers. It had all kinds of edible fruits and was home to all kinds of creatures. The wanderer and its family decided to settle down and become part of the family of this happy tree.

The wanderer was an artist. One day, the wanderer went in search of something to paint and came upon a tree. The tree looked very angry and threatening. Its roots were not deep in the soil and it looked as though it would fall any minute. The wanderer noticed a uniqueness in the tree which was beautiful. The uniqueness was an attractive quality to make the subject of a painting, monumentalise and include in an exhibition. As the wanderer was wondering what to do and how to compose the work, something in the tree made the wanderer feel so uncomfortable, so much that the wanderer's inspiration and enthusiasm dried up. To make the matter worse, the tree appeared to be tilting over towards the wanderer and the wanderer quickly moved away from the tree to avoid being crushed by its weight.

The wanderer continued its walk in search of a subject for its painting. It then came upon another tree with all kinds of butterflies, bees and little beings making it their home. It is a tree of many colours. The wanderer was inspired by the beauty of this tree. The tree appeared to be inviting the wanderer and welcoming it to its home. The wanderer settled down and started to paint enthusiastically. Joy beamed through every part of the wanderer. As the wanderer painted, it noticed that the tree was humming in harmony with the strokes on the canvas. The wanderer's paint brush was even dancing and the wanderer itself joined in the humming. It hummed what the tree hummed. The tree was humming *"Impossible becomes possible, in LOVE all is possible"*. The wanderer was fully energised even though it had not eaten for many hours. The wanderer painted all day and produced a painting full of beauty.

As the wanderer walked home, the wanderer continued to beam with joy and sang aloud. Suddenly, its song was interrupted by a very loud crash! *"What was that? A tree?"* thought the wanderer. Then the wanderer heard the stampede of beings all heading towards the crash. Chanting and stamping in harmony as they raced.

Crash of a tree
Let's go and see
Feast for all
Or sore to see

The sound of the crash had travelled far and near and caused different kinds of beings to race towards the sound of the crash. This is the normal reaction of beings to the sound of a fallen tree. The crash is the tree's own announcement of its transition. The start of a new journey. A change of sorts.

The sound of a fallen tree brings joy to beings just as a baby's first cry brings joy to those expecting the baby's entrance into their world. Beings elatedly race to a fallen tree. A fallen tree is very important to its world. Parts of a fallen tree may be used to make fire. Some parts may become home to ants. Some parts journey to become tables, chairs or musical instruments. Some beings use parts of a fallen tree as materials for writing words. The usefulness of a fallen tree is one reason why beings of all kinds race to a fallen tree. They go to it to celebrate its life with dance, praise singing, music making and story-telling.

The sound of a tree crash has always been a great sound. But this crash was different. It didn't sound quite right but beings followed the sound anyway. Then a strange thing happened. The beings which got to the tree were seen turning away and fleeing from the scene of the crash. The tree had no name and no praise song could be made without a name. Even worse, the tree was releasing bad odour which drove beings away. The disgusting odour was carried by the gentle breeze which does not discriminate. The gentle breeze carried and spread the stench beyond the place where the fallen tree lay. The wanderer perceived the unpleasant odour and ran away from it as fast as it could.

Ebuka perceived the offensive odour and so did that beautiful tree which inspired the painting on the canvas. Both trees knew at once that the wreaking odour is the smell given off by a fallen tree which did not try its best. They knew that a tree which tried its best will give out a beautiful scent following its crash. The beautiful scent will attract wanderers and beings who will then use the tree's trunk, leaves, branches and roots to create beautiful works.

'Something had to be done', Ebuka thought. What Ebuka did next was amazing. Ebuka released its emergency scent to counter the revolting odour. The beautiful tree which inspired the beautiful painting also released an emergency scent. These scents combined to diffuse the reek and restored enriching scents in the environment. The whole space was transformed. The gentle breeze which does not discriminate carried the good scents far and near. All the beings running away from the destructive odour were reached and touched by the good scents. The beings became soothed and relaxed. They stopped running and started breathing in the beautiful fragrance from Ebuka and the tree which inspired the beautiful painting. The wanderer was also touched and energised by the enriching scents. The wanderer ran home without stopping to share its exciting news of the day with Ebuka and the rest of the family.

As the wanderer hung the beautiful painting on one of Ebuka's branches, it continued to hum '*impossible becomes possible, in LOVE all is possible*'. When Ebuka saw the painting, a big smile beamed through Ebuka and spread to its tree-family. Every being touched by Ebuka's smile radiated brilliance never seen before. The painting on the canvas, itself, was beaming smiles and singing "*Impossible becomes possible, in LOVE all is possible*". Ebuka knew at once that Mma had realised its dream.

Ebuka continued to beam a brilliance never seen before and uncontrollably sang out '*Anyo Anyo*'. Mma heard Ebuka's song and was overjoyed. Both have achieved their dreams. Jubilantly, both sang and danced. Despite the distance between them, their songs crossed over the distance to be heard and harmonised in each other's home. They shared their stories and adventures through the crossing exchange of songs. All the beings around joined in the celebrations. The song rose and the dance expanded. The trees shook and the land heaved. The passing cloud turned and its colour changed. The sun smiled and its warmth touched. The gentle breeze cooled and the scents cheered. The wanderer beamed and excitedly painted on its canvas, the stories as told by Ebuka and Mma.

Suddenly the wind arrived at the scene and joined in. It began blowing its trumpet and whistling its special tune. Its special tune was an announcement carried over mountains and seas. The wind was announcing that *Ebuka had come of age*. The refrain was echoed by the sea. Ebuka was dancing, chanting and gyrating ecstatically. The wind's trumpet became louder and was heard across lands, seas and mountains. Then something special happened. Crashing sounds as never heard before assembled and harmonised into a beautiful full-bodied great crash music that erupted from Ebuka. A crash was heard across many lands and seas. It was Ebuka. Ebuka's crash. Ebuka majestically bowed. It majestically bowed out. Its bow was its crash. Ebuka was a beauty in crash as it was in height. The sound was heard near and far.

All kinds of beings followed the sound of the crash to where Ebuka lay. It seemed as though Ebuka was beaming joy and glory. The beam of a tree which did its best with all its breath. Scents of beauty became its present breath. Scents of beauty which had never been sensed before. They seemed to be attending to beautify the beaming Ebuka. Special scents seemed to be emanating from Ebuka to meet and to greet. Perceived by all around, it was a celebration of scents of all kinds.

There was great fun, fanfare and jubilation. The beings attending the crash were beaming with joy and singing with passion. Ebuka lent itself to all beings to do with it as they would. The beautiful aura of the atmosphere elevated the beings into a state of creativity and their creative mode was activated. The beings became creative both in thought and in action. Many created all sorts of beauty. Ebuka gradually changed state and became different forms. Some parts of Ebuka became forms of pianos, cellos, drums and other musical instruments. Other parts became forms of pews, tables and chairs. Stories of Ebuka were written by writers. Some were set in stones. Some were drawn on stones. Wood carvers carved images and others created symbols which told stories. Songs and poems found themselves on parts of Ebuka. A new genre of music came to be named CRASH a short form for 'Ebuka's majestic crash'. Beings named their creations after Ebuka.

Ebuka's beautiful scents remained in the air and continued to be spread by the gentle breeze, the whistling wind, the heaving soil and the cascading sea. Ebuka had changed state. It lived on in the forms of the beings which ate it. It lived on in the forms of the beings which lived in it. It lived on in the forms of the beings which it had become. It lived on in the forms of the beings which had become it, the drums, the beams holding up houses and the leaves carpeting the ground. Forms of Ebuka were not just in one place, they were in all places where Ebuka's wind of change touched and where Ebuka's special scent permeated.

Ebuka had journeyed home to many homes in different forms. To the homes of its dreams. To the homes in its adventures. Its roots had routed through to find the root of its dream. The root of that hard dark quiet place where Ebuka found itself after the storm. The root which became a route.

Forms of Ebuka found a home in that hard dark quiet place where Ebuka found itself after the storm. They felt extraordinarily enriched by making that place their home. The scent Ebuka sensed in that place was the scent Ebuka added to that place. The scent which was a sense. The name of that place and that scent remain unknown because Ebuka never told the name.

Even in a changed form and in different shapes, every season, the different parts of Ebuka harmonised to release pleasant enriching scents. The scents stir something of beauty wherever they touch. The gentle breeze would circulate the scents far and near, beyond each form. In addition, once a year, a special scent is released, a scent not associated with any season. Once released, this scent spreads to reach spaces far and near, permeating wanderers and beings of all kinds. Wanderers are always curious and will set out to find out the source of the scent. They will follow the scent and find themselves in that hard dark quiet place where Ebuka found itself after the storm. Here, the wanderers meet Ebuka, sit on Ebuka, listen to music made from Ebuka, reflect in silence and on thoughts carved on parts of Ebuka. Wanderers love this hard dark quiet place because in it they perceive a soothing presence which always stirred something of beauty in them. In silence, the wanderers, like Ebuka, beam with the beautiful thought of their own dream, energised by the thought of being something, of growing up, of going on adventures, of making their dreams come true. In that silence, something inside of them gets reached, touched and stirred. They get moved and lose themselves, melting into nothingness to expand endlessly in a dream state until the gentle breeze caresses their beings, and transports them to a soil where they could plant their dreams, feed their dreams, live their dreams, become their dreams.

Dreamers always return to forms of Ebuka. Many are moved to return to the form of Ebuka releasing the inspiring scents. At every return, they will share with Ebuka and others their own new stories, the stories of journeys which they completed, the stories of on-going adventures and the stories of their new dreams. Some share these stories in silence. Some share the stories in the form of tears. The wanderers were always free to stop as often as they wanted. So some stopped over at Ebuka's stops at every given opportunity when moved to stop and when things made them to stop in awe.

Names were important to wanderers, so each wanderer touched by Ebuka's scent gave the touch a name informed by how the scent made the wanderer feel. The journeys to parts of Ebuka had also been called different names by different wanderers. Some called it a journey into self. Some called it being in touch with the deep within.

The wanderers used different names to describe that hard dark quiet place where Ebuka found itself after the storm. Some described it as the core. Some called it a place of inspiration. Others described it as the sacred space. One or two had called it the root. Some looked to the hard to name it the silent stone. Others did not give it a name at all but questioned and argued about the description 'silent stone'. How correct is that description? They asked. They said that stone is not the only thing that is hard and questioned whether a stone can be said to be silent. They said that many things about that dark quiet place remains unknown and questioned whether any name is correct when it is likely that many things about that place remain unknown. What do you think? What name would you choose to call that place? That place where Ebuka came alive after the death of the storm. Please share your thoughts.

Did you just ask me about Mma? Oh, Mma is still out there, inspiring wanderers to paint, sing and create beauty. Mma's spirit remains in the gentle breeze stirring beauty to beam all around to reach beings, connect into beings, flow inside beings and become one with beings. Mma and Ebuka still sing together and work in harmony even during crashes of trees which did not try their best. Ebuka works from the inside. Mma works from the outside. Beings continue to relate with all the beauty around and the beauty in each other. So when next you sense a beautiful scent, or see flowers on your path or hear a beautiful sound or music or see trees lining the street or think *"the air is always around me so is my best friend"*, just know that Mma and Ebuka are also around you. They are always enjoying their work, making all kinds of beauties, releasing different beautiful fragrances, diffusing offensive odours, planting smiles on faces, inspiring beings to think.

When next you catch yourself being grumpy, bitter and finding only fault in the ideas of others without proffering any solution to make things better, know that Otumdi has infiltrated your boundaries to make its home in you. You may have knowing or unknowingly eaten Otumdi because we are what we eat.

The thing called Ebuka is that thing inside beings which move beings to connect with the thing outside beings called Mma. When the Ebuka in a being stirs the something inside the being to make connection with the Mma around the being, the connection beams out to make beings smile or flow in tears of awe.

You see beloved one, a thing is as important as a non-thing or a nothing. A being is as important as a non-being. Everything is important and nothing is important. A seen is as important as an unseen. A nameless can become a name. Nothing can become something. Something called Ebuka. Something called Mma. Something called Otumdi.

The something called Ebuka still stirs something of beauty inside beings. The something called Mma still connects with the beauty in beings to make them sing and beam with smiles. Otumdi still storms through beings and still releases offensive odour but thankfully, Ebuka and Mma are always around to diffuse the odour and transform it into something beautiful. Ebuka works deep inside beings. The thing touching the LOVE deep inside so as to glow and radiate through all seasons, beyond all boundaries to connect with the LOVE outside. The LOVE outside, the LOVE Mma bears and radiates.

Different seasons have different exhibitions of beauty which beautify the mind. Admission to these exhibitions is free. The exhibitions are always guaranteed to thrill. The mystery of nothingness when revealed is guaranteed to thrill. Guaranteed to thrill, this song of in and out:

It started with a song and will end in a song
It started with a dance and will end in a dance
It started with an in and will end in an out
It started with a take and will end in a give
It started with a breath and will end in a breath
This breath of in and out
This space of song and dance
A space to be to be
This space of give and take
What have you got to give?
Here is something to share
LOVE TO YOU ALWAYS
LOVE TO ALL ALWAYS

The exhibition is not ended but we return to where we started.

Have you made a name? What's your name you ask? What's my name you ask?

LOVE TO YOU ALWAYS
LOVE TO ALL ALWAYS

WHAT I THOUGHT AT THIS POINT

This is a different approach to making a name
A style different from the style I chose
I like their style
Ebuka, Mma, Otumdi
They observed
Got inspired
Then chose a way to be
And went on to become it
I like the name Ebuka
Mma is beautiful
They became the name they chose

Otumdi did not want to change but change it did
In this space of change everything changes whether or not
they want to change
Some changes must surely happen
Some you can bring about
With your ability to LOVE
Or the disability known as lack of LOVE

I am beginning to understand
I can choose a name at the beginning
Or acquire a name as I go along
Or be given a name by others
Or make myself a name

Or make my name myself

I have not yet decided on what name to bear
What name do you see in me?
Ebuka, Mma, Otumdi?
The enquirer, the wanderer, the listener?
The speaker, the thinker, the reader?
A book, a writing, a writer?
A child, a parent, a stranger?
An artist, a song, a dance?
A breath, a forest, a tree?
The name my father gave me?
The name my mother gave my father?
The name you gave me?

I think I made a name even when I thought I made no name
I made indecision my name when I could not decide on a
name
But now I come to name
In this space where names come to be made
I invoke a name
I have decided on a name
I join the dance of names
I call out my own name
With all the force of joy
I pronounce my own name
With all the breath of jubilation
I name myself after that of which I am made
I call myself by that which is stored in me
I call myself by that name which reflects all I have come to
learn
I am what I am because of what made me
I am made of LOVE, the LOVE stored in me

I am made to LOVE, the LOVE nurturing me
I am what I am because of what is in me
We are what we eat
What I eat is what I am
LOVE nourishes me so LOVE is what I am
I choose MANY LOVERS as my name of now
I choose MANY LOVERS, the name to distinguish me
I choose MANY LOVERS as the name to be called
Call me MANY LOVERS, drum and dance to it
I have Many LOVERS
Many LOVERS are in me
I have Many LOVERS
Many LOVERS made me what I am

What name have you made?
What name has made you?
What shall I call you?